Bahamas

Primary Social Studies

Grade 4

Lisa Greenstein
Karen Morrison

Acknowledgements

Every effort has been made to trace all copyright holders, but if any have been inadvertently overlooked, the Publishers will be pleased to make the necessary arrangements at the first opportunity.

Although every effort has been made to ensure that website addresses are correct at time of going to press, Hodder Education cannot be held responsible for the content of any website mentioned in this book. It is sometimes possible to find a relocated web page by typing in the address of the home page for a website in the URL window of your browser.

Hachette UK's policy is to use papers that are natural, renewable and recyclable products and made from wood grown in well-managed forests and other controlled sources. The logging and manufacturing processes are expected to conform to the environmental regulations of the country of origin.

Orders: please contact Hachette UK Distribution, Hely Hutchinson Centre, Milton Road, Didcot, Oxfordshire, OX11 7HH. Telephone: +44 (0)1235 827827. Email education@hachette.co.uk Lines are open from 9 a.m. to 5 p.m., Monday to Friday. You can also order through our website: www.hoddereducation.com

ISBN: 9781398390089

© Lisa Greenstein and Karen Morrison 2023

First published in 2023 by

Hodder Education,
An Hachette UK Company
Carmelite House
50 Victoria Embankment
London EC4Y 0DZ

www.hoddereducation.com

Impression number   10 9 8 7 6 5 4 3 2 1

Year   2026 2025 2024 2023

Cover photo © Andrea Izzotti – stock.adobe.com

Illustrations by Vian Oelofsen, Stéphan Theron

Typeset in 12 on 16pt FS Albert

Printed in Spain

A catalogue record for this title is available from the British Library.

Text acknowledgements

p.61 source: https://www.grandbahamamuseum.org/exhibits/history-of-the-port-authority/gambling-bahamas; **p. 72** Source: https://www.bahamas.gov.bs/wps/wcm/connect/e1d636dd-1a9b-4661-9e38-ba9bf546a534/FINAL+Bahamas+Fisheries+ % 26+Aquaculture+Sector+Review+17Nov16.pdf?MOD=AJPERES.

Photo acknowledgements

p. 4 *cc*, **p. 6** *cc* © firewings/stock.adobe.com; **p. 5** *cl*, **p. 6** *cc* © Srnicholl/stock.adobe.com; **p. 8** *tr* © Asma Samoh/Shutterstock.com; **p. 9** *cl* © Saidauita/stock.adobe.com; **p. 9** *cl*, **p. 77** *cl* © Daboost/stock.adobe.com; **p. 10** *br* © Cathy T, Junkanoo,Drums/https://creativecommons.org/licenses/by/2.0/legalcode; **p. 14** *tl* © Georgios Kollidas/stock.adobe.com; **p. 17** *tr* © Georgios Kollidas/stock.adobe.com; **p. 17** *bl* © Miriam/stock.adobe.com; **p. 20** *br* © Wangkun Jia/stock.adobe.com; **p. 21** *tr* © prapann/stock.adobe.com; **p. 22** *tl* © tobago77/stock.adobe.com; **p. 23** *cl* SONNET Sylvain/hemis.fr/Alamy Stock Photo; **p. 23** *cc* © Richard Ellis/Alamy Stock Photo; **p. 23** *cc* © Shane Pinder/Alamy Stock Photo; **p. 23** *cr* © Andrey/stock.adobe.com; **p. 24** *tr* © Morphart/stock.adobe.com; **p. 25** *bc* © Archive Images/Alamy Stock Photo; **p. 26** *bc* © Bill Waterson/Alamy Stock Photo; **p. 27** *bl* © Aaron Arrowsmith, Public domain, via Wikimedia Commons; **p. 29** *cc* © Peter Hermes Furian/stock.adobe.com; **p. 30** *bl* © JORDI CAMÍ/Alamy Stock Photo; **p. 31** *cr* © Charles O. Cecil/Alamy Stock Photo; **p. 32** *tl* © The Trustees of the British Museum; **p. 32** © Eric Gaba/https://creativecommons.org/licenses/by-sa/2.0/deed.en; **p. 34** *cr* © D and S Photography Archives/Alamy Stock Photo; **p. 34** *bl* © Archivist/stock.adobe.com; **p. 35** *cc* © GRANGER - Historical Picture Archive/Alamy Stock Photo; **p. 38** *bl* © Makhnach/stock.adobe.com; **p. 39** *cr* © designer_things/stock.adobe.com; **p. 40** *bc* © pbardocz/stock.adobe.com; **p. 41** *bc* © Peter Hermes Furian/stock.adobe.com; **p. 46** *cl* © gizemg/stock.adobe.com; **p. 47** *cl* © olinchuk/stock.adobe.com; **p. 49** *tl* © forcdan/stock.adobe.com; **p. 49** *br* © Tosh Brown/Alamy Stock Photo; **p. 50** *cl* © forcdan/stock.adobe.com; **p. 50** *cc* © sljubisa/stock.adobe.com; **p. 50** *cr* © O Sweet Nature/stock.adobe.com; **p. 59** *tr* © Norman Wharton/Alamy Stock Photo; **p. 60** *cl* © Neil Baylis/Alamy Stock Photo; **p. 60** *cl* © Artokoloro/Alamy Stock Photo; **p. 62** *cl* © Eskystudio/stock.adobe.com; **p. 63** *br* © David Keith Jones/Images of Africa Photobank/Alamy Stock Photo; **p. 64** *cl* © Jeffrey Isaac Greenberg 4+/Alamy Stock Photo; **p. 64** *cr* © Travis VanDenBerg/Alamy Stock Photo; **p. 64** *bl* © Yuka/stock.adobe.com; **p. 64** *br* © BlueOrange Studio/stock.adobe.com; **p. 66** *cl* © SpicyTruffel/stock.adobe.com; **p. 66** *cc* © Mountain Brothers/stock.adobe.com; **p. 67** *cl* © Alex Photo Stock/Shutterstock; **p. 67** *cc* © panuwat/stock.adobe.com; **p. 67** *cl* © Andrey Popov/stock.adobe.com; **p. 67** *cc* © pincasso/stock.adobe.com; **p. 67** *cl* © batuhan toker/stock.adobe.com; **p. 67** *cc* © Rainer Lesniewski/Alamy Stock Vector; **p. 68** *cl* © NAN728/Shutterstock.com; **p. 69** *tr* © dbvirago/stock.adobe.com; **p. 77** *tr* © Ron Buskirk/Alamy Stock Photo; **p. 78** *cl* © Allstar Picture Library Ltd/Alamy Stock Photo; **p. 78** *cc* © Allstar Picture Library Ltd/Alamy Stock Photo; **p. 78** *cc* © Zuma Press, Inc./Alamy Stock Photo; **p. 78** *cc* © Associated Press/Alamy Stock Photo; **p. 78** *cr* © Associated Press/Alamy Stock Photo; **p. 81** *bl* © B O›Kane/Alamy Stock Photo; **p. 87** © Lili Graphie/stock.adobe.com; **p. 92** *cl* © Marc Guitard/Getty Images; **p. 93** © Neil Sealey; **p. 96** *cr* © Derek Brumby/stock.adobe.com; **p. 97** *cc* © saidauita/stock.adobe.com; **p. 102** *cl* © Richard Ellis/Alamy Stock Photo; **p. 103** *cl* © Fanfo/stock.adobe.com; **p. 103** *cc* © Blue Orange Studio/stock.adobe.com; **p. 103** *cc* © Marco Ramerini/stock.adobe.com; **p. 104** *cc* © elvis santana/stock.adobe.com; **p. 104** *cr* © Alina/stock.adobe.com; **p. 104** *cc* © Beautiful textures/stock.adobe.com; **p. 104** *cr* ©Artyponds/stock.adobe.com; **p. 104** *cc* © youli/stock.adobe.com; **p. 104** *cr* © Katy Pavliuk/stock.adobe.com; **p. 105** *tr* © Balint Radu/stock.adobe.com; **p. 105** *cr* © Emmy Ljs/Shutterstock; **p. 105** *cr* © Amphawan/stock.adobe.com; **p. 106** *bc* © SvetlanaSF/Shutterstock.

t = top, *b* = bottom, *l* = left, *r* = right, *c* = centre

Contents

Introduction

Welcome to *Bahamas Primary Social Studies Grade 4*.

The book is divided into three **themes**:
- **Theme 1**   My Bahamian heritage
- **Theme 2**   Our resources and our institutions
- **Theme 3**   Celebrating being Bahamian.

You will work through one theme during each school term. The themes follow the curriculum guidelines set out by the Ministry of Education of The Bahamas.

The **Contents** page before this Introduction helps you to locate the themes and units in this book.

Each theme is divided into various units. Some units are longer than others. Shorter units may take a lesson or two to complete; longer units may take a week or two.

Your teacher will help to guide you through each unit. This is what you will find in each unit:

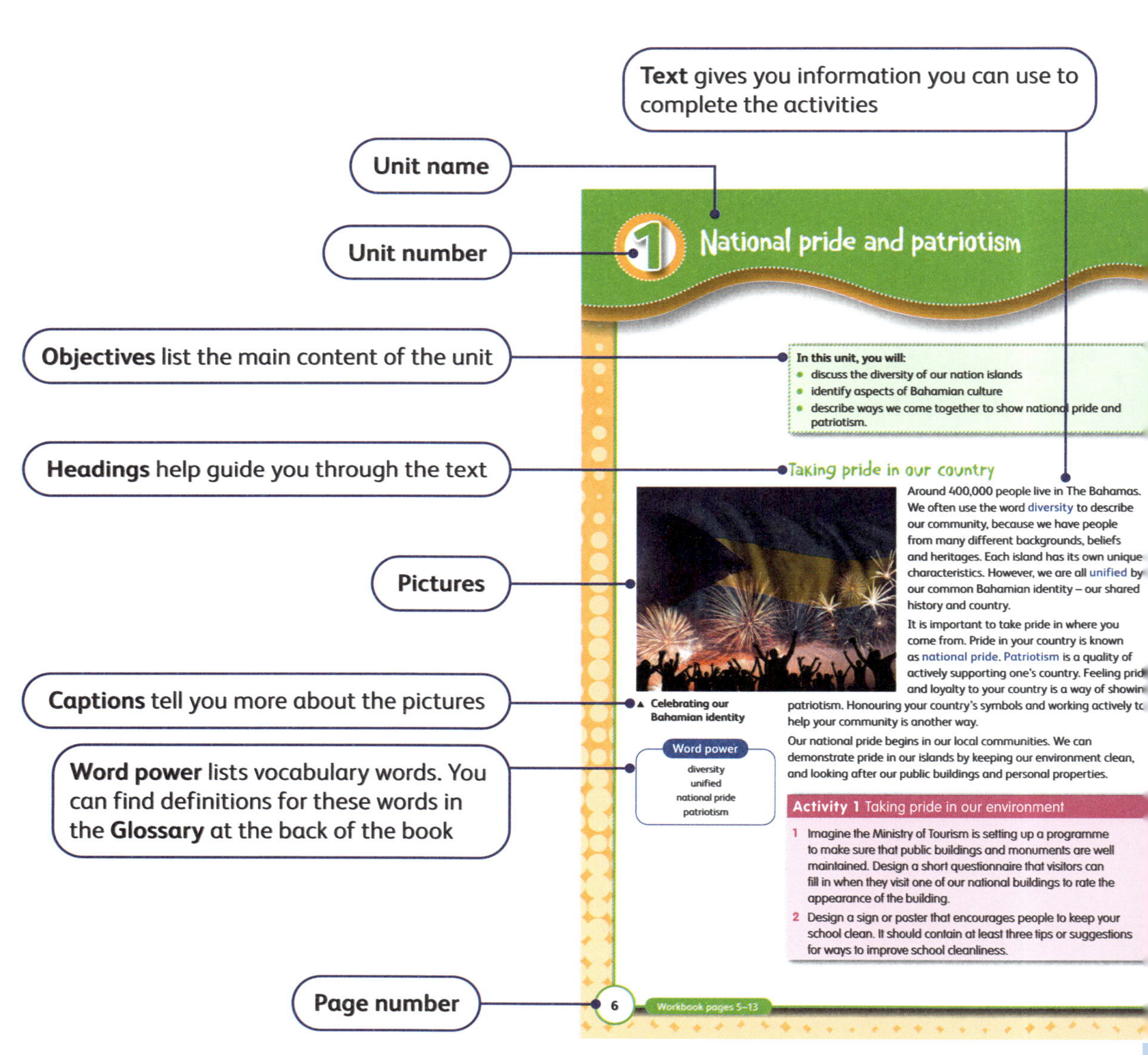

Other features you may notice in a unit are the following:

- **Did you know?** boxes give extra bits of interesting information.
- **Tips** boxes give you extra guidance for your learning.
- **Case study** boxes provide examples of how the ideas you are learning about apply to real-life situations.
- **Reflection** boxes help you to think back over what you have learnt in each unit.

Did you know?

The words potato, canoe, iguana, barbecue, tobacco and hammock were all Taíno words.

Tips

Remember, a percentage is a fraction out of 100. You need to convert your percentages to fractions out of 360 to work out each angle in the pie chart.

Case study

The Old Inhabitants of Long Island

The Bahamas were not empty islands when the Loyalists arrived. The people living here included descendents of early European settlers. The Loyalists looked down on these white Bahamians, who were known as Conchs.

Reflection

What did you find most interesting in this unit? Why?

At the end of each theme, a **What have you learnt?** section helps you to revise the units that were covered in that theme.

Finally, at the end of the book you will find a **Glossary**, with a list of all the word power words and their definitions.

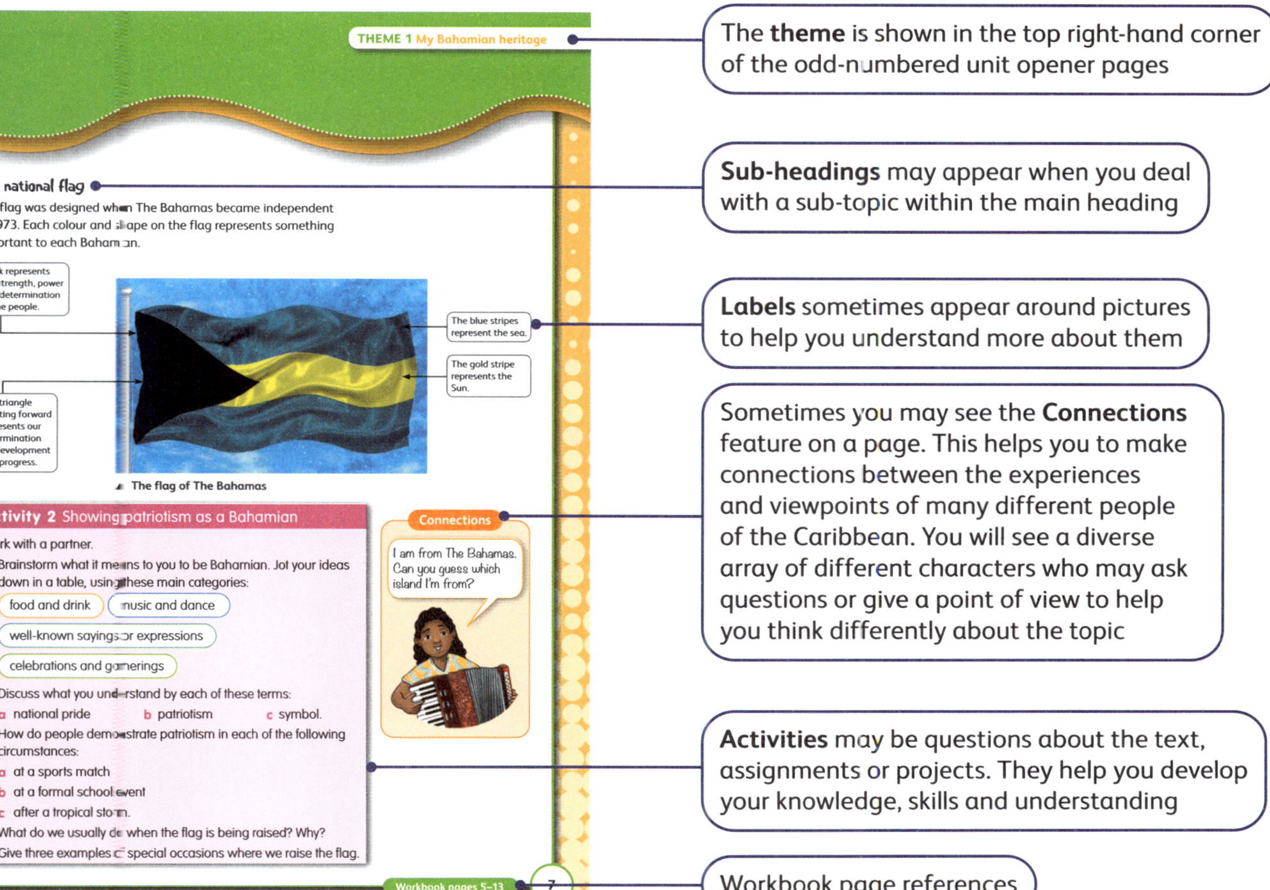

The **theme** is shown in the top right-hand corner of the odd-numbered unit opener pages

Sub-headings may appear when you deal with a sub-topic within the main heading

Labels sometimes appear around pictures to help you understand more about them

Sometimes you may see the **Connections** feature on a page. This helps you to make connections between the experiences and viewpoints of many different people of the Caribbean. You will see a diverse array of different characters who may ask questions or give a point of view to help you think differently about the topic

Activities may be questions about the text, assignments or projects. They help you develop your knowledge, skills and understanding

Workbook page references

1 National pride and patriotism

Taking pride in our country

▲ Celebrating our Bahamian identity

Word power

diversity
unified
national pride
patriotism

Around 400,000 people live in The Bahamas. We often use the word **diversity** to describe our community, because we have people from many different backgrounds, beliefs and heritages. Each island has its own unique characteristics. However, we are all **unified** by our common Bahamian identity – our shared history and country.

It is important to take pride in where you come from. Pride in your country is known as **national pride**. **Patriotism** is a quality of actively supporting one's country. Feeling pride and loyalty to your country is a way of showing patriotism. Honouring your country's symbols and working actively to help your community is another way.

Our national pride begins in our local communities. We can demonstrate pride in our islands by keeping our environment clean, and looking after our public buildings and personal properties.

Activity 1 Taking pride in our environment

1 Imagine the Ministry of Tourism is setting up a programme to make sure that public buildings and monuments are well maintained. Design a short questionnaire that visitors can fill in when they visit one of our national buildings to rate the appearance of the building.

2 Design a sign or poster that encourages people to keep your school clean. It should contain at least three tips or suggestions for ways to improve school cleanliness.

The national flag

Our flag was designed when The Bahamas became independent in 1973. Each colour and shape on the flag represents something important to each Bahamian.

▲ **The flag of The Bahamas**

Activity 2 Showing patriotism as a Bahamian

Work with a partner.

1 Brainstorm what it means to you to be Bahamian. Jot your ideas down in a table, using these main categories:

food and drink   music and dance

well-known sayings or expressions

celebrations and gatherings

2 Discuss what you understand by each of these terms:
   a national pride   b patriotism   c symbol.

3 How do people demonstrate patriotism in each of the following circumstances:
   a at a sports match
   b at a formal school event
   c after a tropical storm.

4 What do we usually do when the flag is being raised? Why?

5 Give three examples of special occasions where we raise the flag.

Connections

Our Coat of Arms and our motto

A **Coat of Arms** is a type of symbolic crest or emblem. It is an image composed of several different important symbols including the yellow elder (our national flower), the *Lignum vitae* (our national tree), the pink flamingo (our national bird) and the blue marlin (our national fish). At the bottom of the Coat of Arms you can also read the national motto.

Word power

Coat of Arms

▶ The Coat of Arms of The Bahamas

Activity 3 The Coat of Arms and motto

1 Identify five other things you can see on the Coat of Arms. Explain why you think they were included.
2 Write the words of the motto, and explain its meaning.

Activity 4 An island crest

Imagine that you have been given the task of designing a crest for your particular island.

1 Think of things that are unique to your island. They may be plants or animals, places, landmarks or symbols of events from the past or the present.
2 Design your own Coat of Arms. Around your design, write what each thing represents.

Tips

You can draw the images, or cut out pictures from tourist brochures or magazines, and stick them together to make your Coat of Arms. Or you can create your image electronically on a computer or tablet.

The national anthem and pledge

Each country has its own **national anthem** – a song that is sung at official events and conveys the spirit of all the people who live in that country. Our anthem was composed by Timothy Gibson when The Bahamas achieved independence.

March on, Bahamaland

Lift up your head to the rising sun, Bahamaland;
March on to glory, your bright banners waving high.
See how the world marks the manner of your bearing!
Pledge to excel through love and unity.

Pressing onward, march together
to a common loftier goal;
Steady sunward, tho' the weather
hide the wide and treacherous shoal.

Lift up your head to the rising sun, Bahamaland,
'Til the road you've trod lead unto your God,

March on, Bahamaland!

The Bahamas also has a national **pledge**.

I *pledge* my *allegiance* to the *flag* and to the
Commonwealth of *The Bahamas*
For which it stands, one people *united* in love and service.

Activity 5 The anthem and pledge

1 **a** As a class, recite the words of the pledge and the anthem.

   b Discuss what the words in *italic* letters mean. What does it ask of us?

   c Practise singing the national anthem.

2 Choose either the pledge or the national anthem. Create a cartoon strip that illustrates or depicts the words. If you have access to a drawing or animation program on a computer or tablet, you can create a digital animation.

Aspects of Bahamian culture

What do we mean when we talk about Bahamian culture? Read what these different Bahamians say about the word 'culture'.

What makes life in The Bahamas different to life in other countries? Think about our language and expressions, how we dress, our greetings, our cuisine, and our style of music, art and dance.

Activity 6 Comparing my island to another

1. Identify your island on a map in your atlas, or the map on page 42 of this book. Then identify the three islands nearest to yours.
2. Choose another island. Make a chart to compare it to yours. Compare:
   - geography (land size and shape, climate and vegetation)
   - people (population size and which areas have the most people)
   - important events and celebrations
   - any other similarities and differences.

▲ **Junkanoo is celebrated widely in The Bahamas**

Reflection

What did you find most interesting in this unit? Why?

2 The Lucayans and the arrival of Columbus

In this unit, you will:
- define colony, freedom and religion
- identify how the Lucayans contributed to our culture
- describe the impact of Columbus' arrival.

Who were the Lucayans?

The Lucayans lived in The Bahamas from around 700 AD until about 1500 AD. They shared ancestors with the Taíno groups on other Caribbean islands. We still use many words from their language and culture.

We know about the Lucayans from different **sources**. **Archaeologists** have found **artefacts**, such as bones, pottery, shells and tools on many islands. We also have **first-hand accounts** from explorers who met the Lucayans. All these sources give us an idea of what Lucayan life was like.

> **Word power**
> source
> archaeologist
> artefact
> first-hand account
> dugout canoe

▲ The drawings in this chapter give an artist's impression of Lucayan life in The Bahamas

Lucayans were excellent sailors and fishermen. They built their own **dugout canoes** so that they could travel to different islands and trade. More than 70 people could fit into one canoe. They mostly caught and ate fish, such as parrotfish, grouper, snapper and other bony fishes. They also ate crabs, clams, conch, turtles and monk seals. They caught their seafood in many ways – using spears, bows and arrows, weirs, nets and basket traps. Sometimes they ate land animals, such as iguana and hutia (a local rodent). They barbecued their meat and fish.

> **Did you know?**
> The words potato, canoe, iguana, barbecue, tobacco and hammock were all Taíno words.

The Lucayans grew many different crops, including sweet and bitter manioc (cassava), sweet potatoes, yams, beans and gourds, chilli peppers, guava, papaya and agave. They also grew cotton and tobacco, which they used and traded with neighbours. They made a living from trading their crops and from fishing.

Did you know?

The Spanish explorers had never seen hammocks before they met the Lucayans. They liked the idea so much that they began using hammocks on their ships. They also took the idea back to Europe.

Many families lived and worked together in large huts. They used palm leaves for thatch. Rectangular-shaped huts were called caney, and oval-shaped huts were called bohio. Each hut held several dozen families. The men were often away on trading trips, so the households were centred around mothers, grandmothers, sisters and daughters.

They stored their belongings on the floor or up in the rafters, and slept in cotton hammocks.

Word power

cacique
duho

Lucayans also had their own system of government. The chief was called the **cacique**. He lived in a hut in a special position in the village. The cacique usually had a special chair called a **duho**, carved in the shape of a man crouching on all fours.

Activity 1 Brainstorm using a graphic organiser

Graphic organisers are any type of diagram that arranges text and shapes in a way that helps you to understand, organise or remember how the information fits together. One example is a **mind map**. You write your topic or question in the middle, and arrange shapes around it, listing different categories. Then you jot down your ideas around each category.

Work in groups to brainstorm the things we do or use today that come from our Lucayan ancestors. You can copy the mind map below and add to it, or design your own.

Word power

graphic organiser
mind map

Words that come from the Taíno language

Things they used in everyday life

Contributions of the Lucayans

Culture

Foods

Activity 2 Research Lucayan artefacts

For this activity, you will need internet access.

1   Do an image search for 'Lucayan artefacts'. Find at least three examples of artefacts that were made by Lucayan people or left as remains of their lives here.

2   Draw or print a picture of what you found. Write a short description of what it is, and what it tells us about the Lucayans.

Activity 3 Symbols in the Cacique Awards

Research the Cacique Awards.

1   Write a brief description explaining what the Cacique Awards are.

2   How many different categories are there? Give three examples of nomination categories.

3   What symbols do the Cacique awards use that come from Lucayan culture?

Christopher Columbus was a European sailor and explorer born in the 1400s. Unlike most sailors of his time, he believed the world was round. He wanted to explore new routes to the lands then known as 'the Indies' – China, India and Japan. The king and queen of Spain believed these voyages were opportunities for the Spanish to trade with wealthy lands, and to spread Christianity.

The impact of Columbus in the Caribbean

Christopher Columbus set sail from Spain in August 1492. He had a fleet of three ships – the María, the Niña and the Pinta. By October, he reached an island the Lucayans called Guanahani. Columbus renamed it San Salvador. He believed these islands were part of India, which is why he called them 'the West Indies'.

When the Spanish ships arrived, about 40,000 Lucayans lived in The Bahamas. They welcomed the explorers with gentle curiosity. From Columbus's diaries, we know that the Lucayans swam to the ships, bringing useful things to trade. Columbus noticed that they only used javelins and spears for hunting and fishing. They did not use weapons. The Spanish, however, brought great destruction to the Lucayans and other Taíno.

Without knowing it, Spanish ships brought an invisible killer: diseases that were common in Europe but new to the islands. These arrival of diseases like smallpox, malaria and influenza led to epidemics that wiped out huge numbers of indigenous people throughout the West Indies, and on both continents of America.

Besides these diseases, the Spanish also brought violence and oppression. They did not view Lucayans as human beings. The Spanish committed many violent crimes against the Lucayans and other Taíno. They forced them to work in the gold mines, or transported them back to Spain to be sold as slaves. They also tortured and killed Lucayan people for sport.

The island people had no way to defend themselves against the violence of the Spanish. Within 25 years, the Lucayan society of the islands was gone.

Activity 4 Columbus's route across the Atlantic

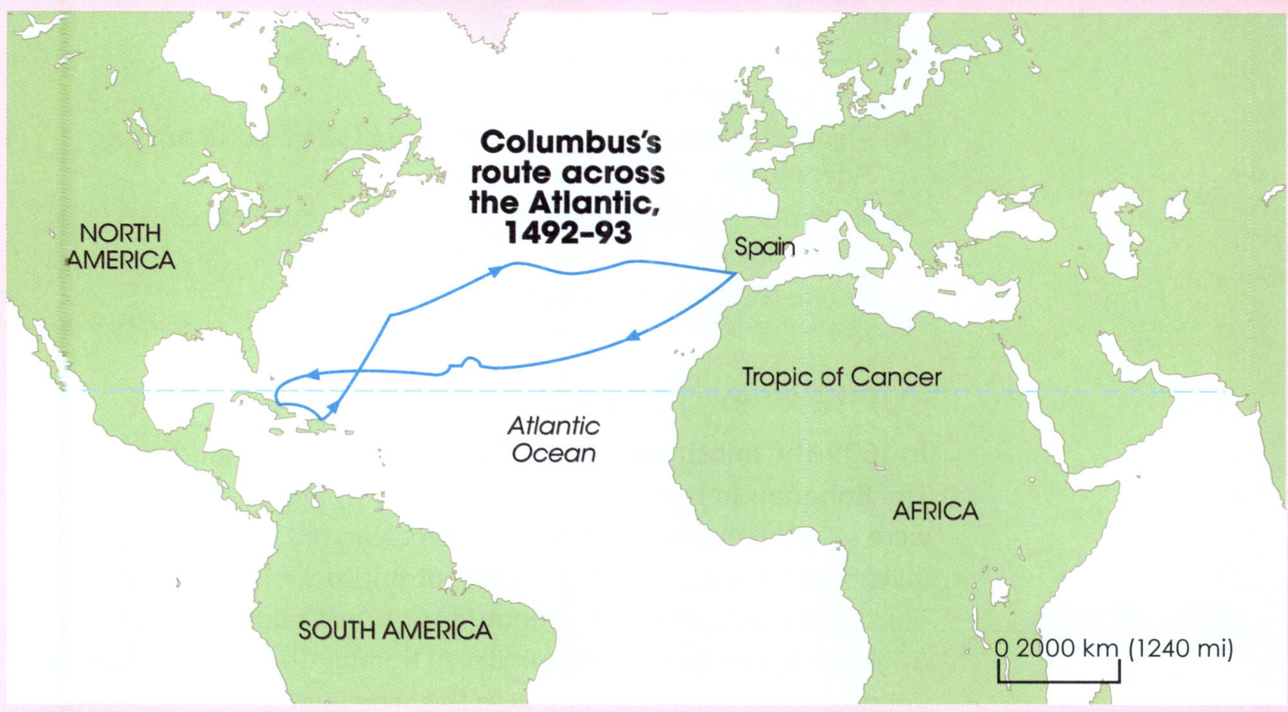

▲ **Columbus's route across the Atlantic**

1 Look at a globe showing the world. Locate India, Spain and The Bahamas.

2 Explain to a partner why Columbus thought he could reach India by sailing west from Spain.

Activity 5 Impact of Columbus's arrival

Imagine that it is 1493, the year after Columbus's arrival in The Bahamas. How would you feel about the arrival of the Spanish? Write a response from two different points of view:

1 the point of view of a Lucayan child

2 the point of view of one of the sailors on the Pinta.

Did you know?

DNA studies show that modern-day populations in South America are descendants of the same Taíno people that the Lucayans came from.

Reflection

Identify which historical event in this unit surprised you the most. Give reasons.

In this unit, you will:
- identify events that led to the arrival of the Eleutheran Adventurers
- recognise the influence of the Eleutheran Adventurers on our society
- define the term plantation.

Puritans in Bermuda

In 1609, the British sent settlers to the island of Bermuda, northwest of The Bahamas in the Atlantic Ocean. By the mid-1600s, however, there were religious and political conflicts breaking out, both in Britain and in its colonies. King Charles I ruled that British subjects should practise Christianity according to the **doctrines** of the Church of England, an Anglican denomination very similar to Roman Catholicism. However, not all British subjects agreed with this. The Puritans were a Protestant denomination with different beliefs to the Anglicans.

Word power

doctrine

Activity 1 The beliefs of the Puritans

Read what these Puritans say about their beliefs. Do a short role play dramatising a conversation between a supporter of King Charles I and a Puritan living in Bermuda in the 1600s.

The journey of the Eleutheran Adventurers

In 1647, a small group of British Puritans in Bermuda refused to swear allegiance to the Anglican King Charles. They formed a company called The Eleutheran Adventurers, led by William Sayle. In 1648 they set sail from Bermuda on a ship called William, and a small boat.

They named the island where they arrived Eleuthera (from the Greek word for freedom). They named their landing place Governor's Harbour. However, Captain Butler had a disagreement with William Sayle, and the company split up. Sayle's party took the small boat and went further along the north coast of the island, but it hit a reef. Shipwrecked, and with all supplies lost, Sayle's party was stranded. They took shelter in a cave, where they held their first church service. This became known as Preacher's Cave.

▲ King Charles I

Activity 2 Interview Sayle or Butler

1   Imagine that you were alive at the time of the Eleutheran arrival. Dramatise an interview with Sayle or Butler. The interview should show that you understand why the Eleutherans came to The Bahamas.

2   What do you understand by the terms below? Write a sentence or two to explain each term in relation to the Eleutherans:

   a colony   **b** religion   **c** freedom.

◄ **People can still visit Preacher's Cave on Eleuthera**

Impact of the Eleutheran Adventurers

The Eleutherans struggled to survive. At first they had only berries and plants to eat. They nearly starved to death. Crops did not grow easily because the soil was very poor. Eventually they set sail for Virginia, where the settlers gave them a ship and some supplies.

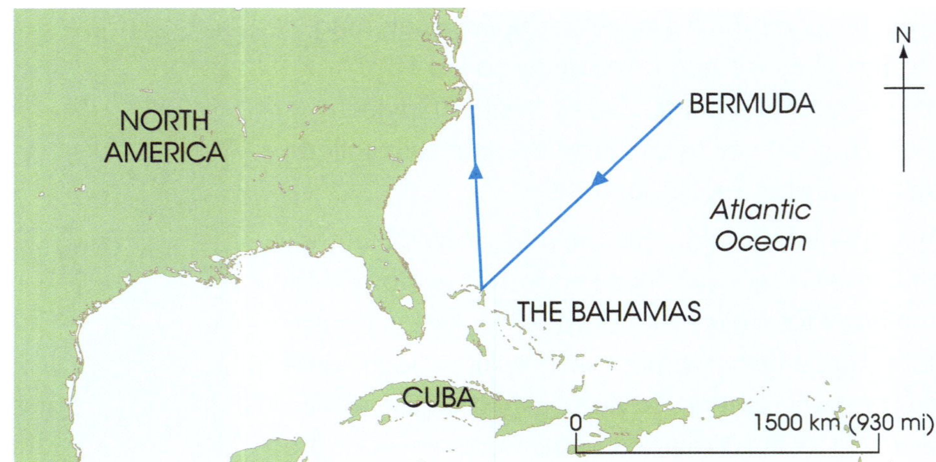

Did you know?

The Eleutherans received support and assistance from settlers in New England. In return, the Eleutherans sent ten tons of brasiletto timber, which were used in the building of Harvard College.

▶ **The route taken by the Eleutheran Adventurers in 1648**

Connections

Family names that come from settler families:

- Albury
- Bethel
- Bullard
- Butler
- Cartwright
- Culmer
- Knowles
- Nottage
- Pinder
- Sands
- Thompson
- Williams

Life on Eleuthera was very hard. In the 1650s, more settlers came from Bermuda. Many of them were criminals. The Puritans did not want to accept them into the community. Food was scarce. The Eleutherans survived by farming and fishing, and also trading timber. They also collected goods from shipwrecked vessels. Eventually, most of the Eleutheran Adventurers either returned to Bermuda or moved to America. Those who stayed eventually moved to join a new settlement on another island, which they called Sayle Island.

Life on Sayle Island was easier than on Eleuthera. It was more sheltered. It also had a good harbour and a more central position. The waters around the island were excellent for fishing, and the land more fertile for farming. This new location brought new hope to the Puritans. They renamed it Providence, and it later became New Providence. The main town was called Charles Town after King Charles I, but it was later renamed Nassau, after William of Nassau.

Reflection

What was the main thing the Eleutheran Adventurers wanted in The Bahamas?

4 The Loyalists

In this unit, you will:
- identify events that led to the Loyalists' arrival
- explain who the Loyalists were
- discuss their impact on The Bahamas, including slavery.

The American Revolution

By the mid-1700s, Britain controlled 13 colonies along the east coast of America. From 1775 until 1783, these colonies fought a war that became known as the American War of Independence, or the American Revolution. Their aim was to be independent of British rule.

However, some of the settlers were still loyal to Britain. They considered themselves British, not American. This group was known as Loyalists. They were loyal to the British empire. They mostly came from the newer, southern colonies of South Carolina and Georgia, where they farmed cotton and tobacco. They had close trade links to Britain. To avoid taking part in the American Revolution, many Loyalists moved to East Florida, which had been under British rule since 1763.

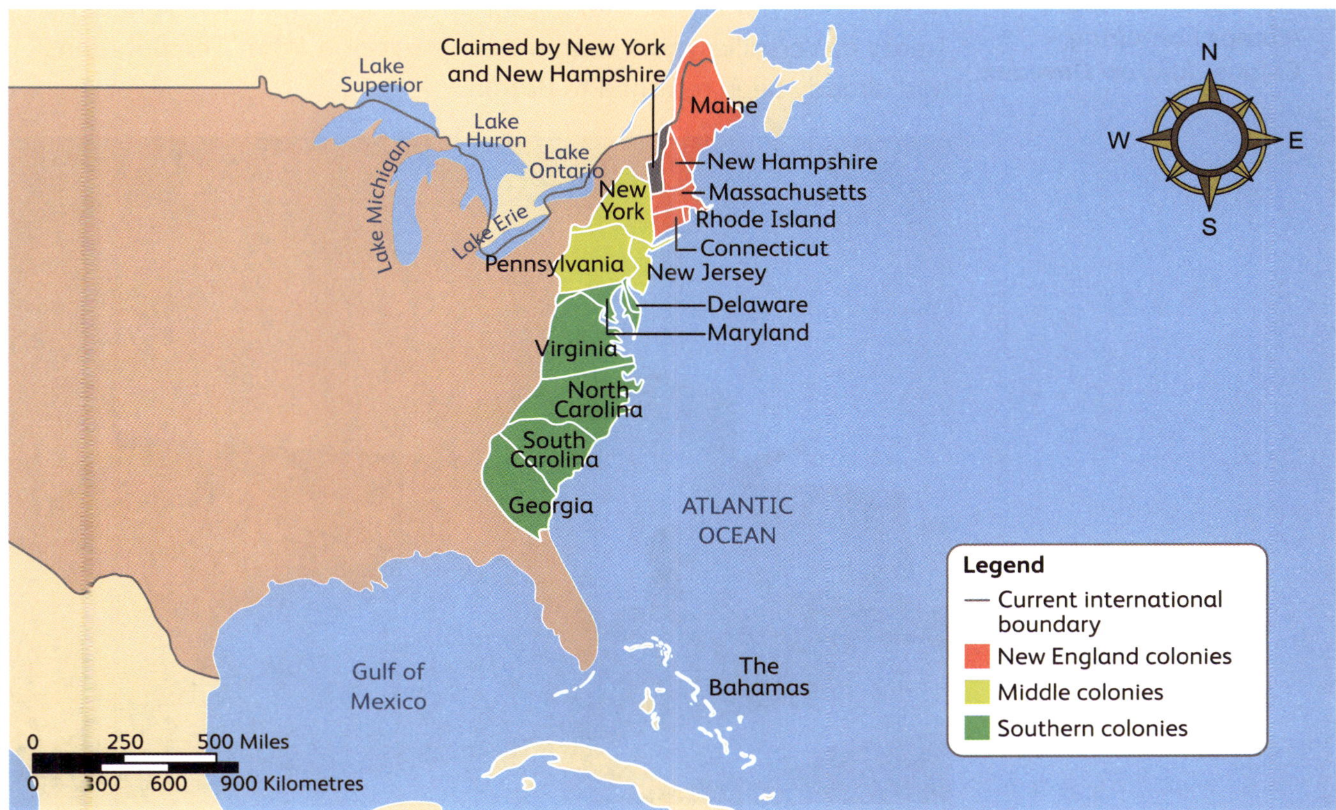

▲ The colonies of the United States at the time of the American Revolution

Involvement of The Bahamas

The Bahamas is very near to the coast of America, where the War of Independence was unfolding. However, The Bahamas was still a loyal British colony.

The American navy attacked The Bahamas several times during the war. They seized supplies of gunpowder and also took Fort Nassau. Eventually in 1782 a Loyalist from East Florida, Colonel Andrew Deveaux, devised a plan to defend The Bahamas from the Americans. By then, the Americans had the support of Spain, who sent their troops to The Bahamas to help occupy the islands.

Deveaux cleverly made it look as though he had far more men than he did – by hiding them in the bottom of a boat, and then rowing them ashore, then returning with the same group hidden, and repeating this many times, as though he were bringing more and more troops. Once on land, he instructed his soldiers to make loud noises so they sounded like a large army. However, many of the 'soldiers' the Spanish saw on Society Hill, overlooking the fort, were in fact made of straw-stuffed uniforms! Scared off by the seeming large numbers of troops, the Spanish surrendered.

Deveaux did not realise that in fact Britain and Spain had signed the Treaty of Versailles more than a week earlier, and that The Bahamas had already been returned to Britain.

▲ **In the 1980s, The Bahamas issued stamps honouring Colonel Andrew Deveaux**

▲ **Fort Montagu**

Who were the Loyalists?

By 1783, America was independent of Britain, and the Treaty of Versailles gave East Florida back to Spain. At the same time, in The Bahamas, the Governor Woodes Rogers was trying to attract more settlers to the islands. To encourage the Loyalists to move to The Bahamas, the British government offered **land grants**.

The promise of free land in a British-ruled country was very attractive to the Loyalists. Many of them moved to The Bahamas. They also brought thousands of enslaved people. The population of The Bahamas rose from around 4000 people in 1783 to more than 11000 by 1789. Most of these people were slaves. Some Loyalists were carpenters, boat builders, fishermen or merchants. But most of them established farms where they could grow crops to sell back to the British. This system achieved great wealth for the Loyalists, but not for the enslaved people, who worked as forced, free labour in the fields and the homes of the Loyalists.

Most Loyalists settled on the largest central and southern islands, which had the most fertile soil for growing cotton. Abaco attracted the most settlers, but Long Island, Exuma, Acklins, Cat Island (still known then as San Salvador), Crooked Island, Eleuthera and San Salvador (then known as Watlings) all became home to large cotton plantations. The Loyalists were Anglicans. They built many churches.

> "To every head of a family, forty acres; and to every white or black man, woman or child in a family, twenty acres, at an annual rent of 2 shillings per hundred acres. But in the case of the Loyalist refugees from the continent, such lands are to be delivered free of charge."

Word power

land grant
architecture

Connections

Activity 1 Events leading to the arrival of the Loyalists

Read the information on pages 19 to 21 to help you complete this activity.

1 Explain the origin of the name Loyalist.
2 Draw a flow chart mapping out the events that led to the arrival of the Loyalists in The Bahamas.

Activity 2 Compare and contrast Loyalists and Eleutheran Adventurers

The Loyalists were different to the Eleutheran Adventurers in several ways. List at least five differences. Use these points to help you:

- date of arrival
- attitude to the King of England
- religious beliefs
- type of farming they did
- how many people they brought to The Bahamas.

Loyalist contributions to The Bahamas

Religious contributions

The Loyalists were proud supporters of the British empire, and practised Christianity in keeping with the Anglican Church (Church of England). They brought the Anglican style of church-building to the islands, which you can still see in churches such as Christ Church Cathedral, St Matthew's Church and St. Patrick's Church.

▶ St. Patrick's Church in Governor's Harbour

Loyalist architecture

The Loyalists established huge cotton farms called **plantations**. A plantation usually had a grand main house where the owner lived with their family. Their buildings followed the Georgian style which was popular in Britain. You can see the same style in plantation houses in New England and the Carolinas. Some traits of this style include:

- symmetrical appearance and classical proportions
- double-storey design (a ground floor and an upstairs)
- a grand entrance with arches or columns
- fanlight windows over a central front door
- painted window shutters
- multi-pane sash windows
- rooms with high ceilings, and details such as mouldings and cornices.

Store rooms and servants' quarters were usually on the ground floor, while the main living rooms and bedrooms for the owner's family were on the first floor. The kitchen was usually separate from the house, so that the owner's family did not need to notice cooking smells and heat, or the work of the servants. Around the house there might be gardens for the family to enjoy. Beyond the house were the cotton fields. Further away from the main house were small, very basic huts for the enslaved people.

Word power

plantation

Did you know?

Many ship carpenters in The Bahamas also worked building houses. This resulted in houses that looked like boats. They had to use materials available in the Caribbean, such as timber. They also designed features to suit the climate, such as a shaded porch around the ground floor and balconies upstairs.

Activity 3 Loyalist architecture

1 Discuss with a partner what similarities and differences you notice about the houses in these pictures.

2 Identify buildings on or near your island built during the Loyalist period. If possible, visit the building or look at pictures. Identify which characteristics made it typical of the Loyalist style.

▲ Loyalist house

▲ Balcony house, Nassau

▲ Deveaux Plantation house, Cat Island

▲ Ruins of Clifton Plantation

Other contributions

Aside from the plantation system, the Anglican religion and their distinctive architecture, the Loyalists had many other influences on Bahamian society.

They believed in the importance of education and built many new schools. One Loyalist settler, John Wells, brought a printing press to the islands, and established the first newspaper in Nassau, *The Gazette.*

The Loyalists also contributed to the **infrastructure** of the islands: they built streets and a new jail, and they set up a police force. Previously, most settlers lived on the islands of New Providence, Eleuthera and Harbour Island. The Loyalists settled many other islands, and five new members were elected to the House of Assembly to represent these islands.

> **Word power**
>
> infrastructure

Activity 4 Loyalist surnames

1 Here are some typical surnames of Loyalist families: Adderley, Bowe, Culmer, Curry, Dean, Ferguson, Forbes, Fox, Johnson, Kelly, Rolle and Russell. Do you recognise any of these surnames? Try to find these surnames in one of the following places:

- a local newspaper
- local street names
- the tombstones at a local cemetery
- names of students or teachers at your school.

2 Make a poster for your classroom titled 'Loyalist surnames on our island today', showing what you found out.

Plantation life and slaves

▶ **An illustration of slave workers in the cotton fields**

Growing cotton requires an enormous amount of hard labour. A single plantation owner could own between 50 and 100 enslaved people. These enslaved people usually had to work from very early in the morning until very late at night.

Field slaves worked in the plantation fields. The work changed with the seasons. First, they would dig and weed the land to prepare it for the cotton crop. Later, they planted the cotton seeds. Through the growing season, they tended to the crops to keep them watered and weeded. Finally, during the busy 'picking season', they picked off the cotton pods and put these through a cotton gin to remove the seeds. Then they packed the cotton into bales to be transported away and sold.

House slaves worked in the main house, doing cooking, housework, washing and cleaning, and looking after their owners' children.

Other enslaved people might also be put to work doing other jobs for their owners, such as hunting, fishing, other farm labour, construction work, or helping in the owner's business or trade.

Enslaved people were obliged to do any menial work that their owners required of them, and they did not have any rights or protections. Slave owners could punish, torture or even kill their slaves if they felt displeased with them.

> **Word power**
>
> field slave
> house slave

To many people, the word 'slave' is dehumanising. By using the term 'enslaved people' we remember that slaves were people who had their rights violated when they were kidnapped and sold into slavery.

Activity 5 A day in the life

1 The picture below shows a cotton plantation in the southern states of America. Plantations in The Bahamas looked very similar to this. In groups, discuss what each person is doing, and what their lives might have been like.

2 Imagine that it is 1785. You live on a plantation. Each student takes a different character (the slave owner, his wife, a field slave, a house slave, a poor white artisan, or any other characters from this time). Dramatise 'a day in the life' of these characters.

Tips

As you do this work, try to imagine fully what it was like to live during this time. Imagine how each person felt, and what struggles and difficulties they may have had in their daily lives. Many of their experiences may be difficult to imagine, or very upsetting to think about. Pay close attention to your own feelings, and the feelings of others. Think of ways you can bring compassion and empathy to this task.

▲ A depiction of a day on a cotton plantation

Old Inhabitants and land grants

For many years, historians believed that many of the islands (besides Eleuthera, Governor's Harbour, New Providence and Abaco) had no one living there until the arrival of the Loyalists. But later, people began to ask: What happened during the period between the destruction of the Lucayans in the early 1500s and the arrival of the American Loyalists around 1783? Were the islands really 'unpeopled'?

Recent research suggests that in fact there were already inhabitants on Long Island by at least 1776, and some possibly as early as 1740. According to some records, more than half the land grants for Long Island went to people who had established a life in The Bahamas long before the arrival of the Loyalists. Historians refer to these people as Old Inhabitants.

▲ A map of Carolina, Florida and the Bahama Islands with the adjacent parts from **The Natural History of Carolina, Florida, and the Bahama Islands (1754) by Mark Catesby (1683–1749)**

Why did the Loyalists think the islands were uninhabited?

Some of the Old Inhabitants were established in The Bahamas, but fled to Florida in 1782, during the brief period when the Spanish took over the islands. They then returned a year later, between 1783 and 1784, together with the Loyalist settlers, although they were not in fact part of Loyalist settler society. Many of these Old Inhabitants were noted in the old land records as free 'black', 'mulatto' or 'coloured' people.

Activity 6 Research Old Inhabitants of The Bahamas

1 For this activity, you will need internet access. Go to the website of Long Island Bahamas History.

   a Under 'Grantees', look for the list of Old Inhabitants.

   b The records on this website show that the spellings of some names changed over time. Give examples of at least two different surnames that have a range of spellings.

   c Choose a surname that is familiar to you from your family or community.

2 Use the website to find out some facts about that family. Report back to your class with what you found out.

◄ An extract from a map drawn in 1803 showing some of the islands of The Bahamas at the time of the Loyalists

Reflection

What was the legacy of the Loyalists? What did they bring to The Bahamas that still forms part of our life here today?

In this unit, you will:

- research some African societies from which our African ancestors came
- define terms: slave, slavery, emancipation, the Middle Passage, freedom
- locate places where enslaved people lived in The Bahamas
- identify ways that African practices shaped Bahamian traditions and culture.

African kingdoms of our ancestors

Africa is the second largest continent after Asia. It is also the place where humankind first evolved tens of thousands of years ago, before humans migrated to the Middle East, Asia, Europe and the Americas.

Between the 1500s and late 1800s, slave traders kidnapped and uprooted millions of people from Africa and brought them into slavery. These enslaved people came from ancient and complex societies on the African continent.

Before we study the slave trade that brought our ancestors across from Africa, it is important to consider the vast size of this continent and the many different cultures and societies that date back many centuries.

Activity 1 What do you know about Africa?

Many people mistakenly think that Africa is a country. In fact, it is a huge continent, with 54 different countries. Divide your class into five groups. Each group discusses one of the regions – north, west, central, eastern or southern Africa.

1 Identify the countries in your chosen region.

2 Compare the map opposite to a physical map (a map showing rivers, mountains and other natural features). Identify some rivers in the region that form the borders between some of the countries.

3 In your group, discuss what you know about the countries in the region you have chosen. What do you think of when you hear these place names? What do you think life is like there? Do you know of anyone who comes from this country, or anything that has happened there?

4 Choose one or more of the countries to focus on. Look in reference books or online and find out about the country and its people. Report back to the class five facts you learnt.

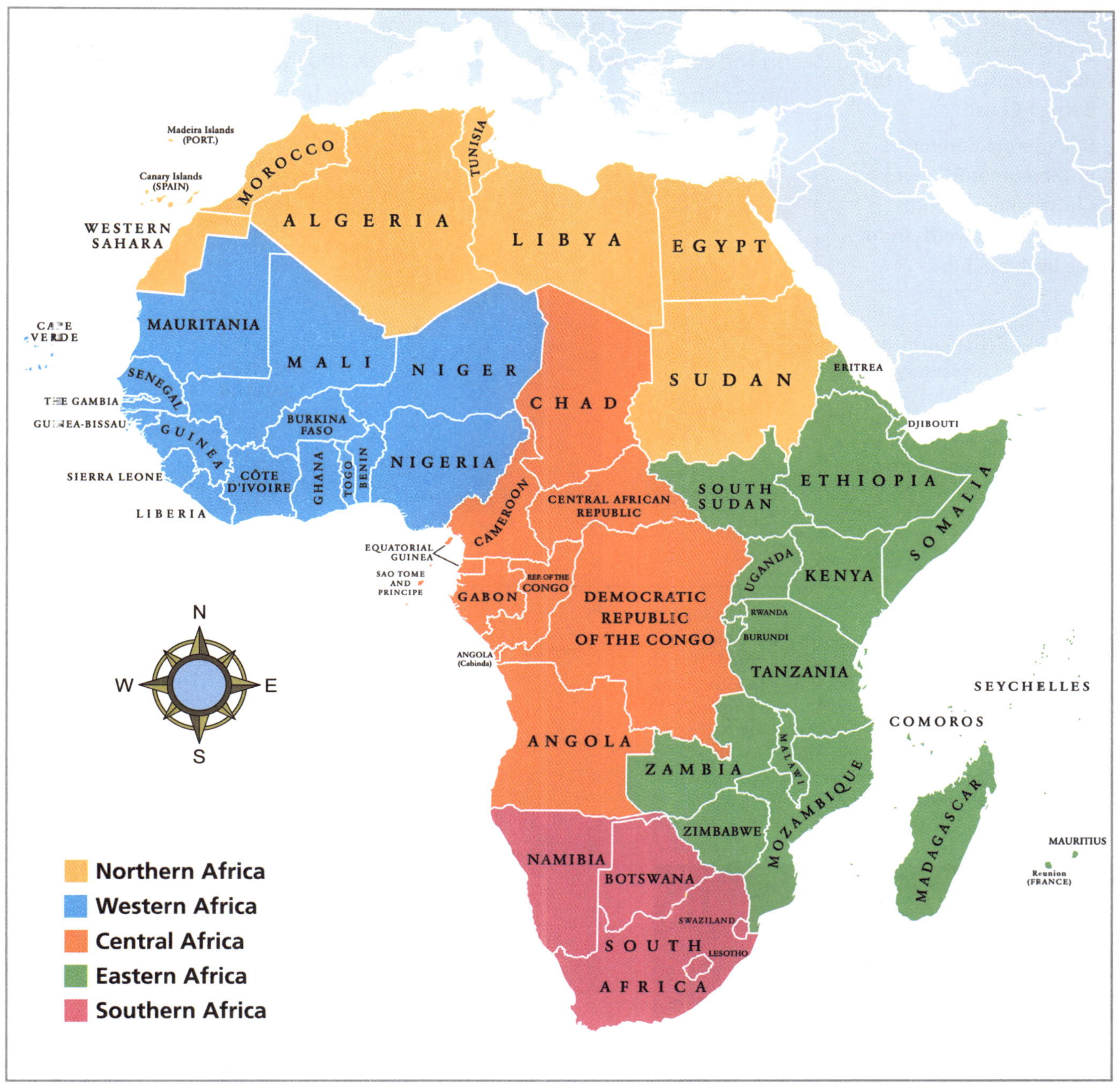

▲ Because Africa is made up of so many countries, we sometimes group them together. Our ancestors were enslaved people from the western and central regions of Africa

Ancient societies in Africa

There are not many written records from Africa's ancient civilisations. Historians use archaeological evidence and oral histories to study African history. There are hundreds of different civilisations that arose on the African continent. Here are a few that were powerful in West Africa, the region that our ancestors come from.

> **Tips**
>
> CE (Common Era), also sometimes AD (Anno Domini, meaning 'in the year of the Lord) refers to dates measured from the birth of Christ.
>
> BCE (Before Common Era) or sometimes BC (Before Christ) refers to dates counted backwards from the birth of Christ.

From the 6th century CE (the years 501–600) until around the 13th century, the Ghana Empire was very powerful in West Africa. It was located over parts of the countries today known as Mauritania and Mali. Rich supplies of iron, copper, gold and ivory in this part of Africa made the people of this empire very successful at trading with other African societies as well as Europe. From the 1400s, it would become part of the Mali Empire.

The Mali Empire was established by King Sundiata Keita, uniting several smaller kingdoms located around the Upper Niger Area. Between the 13th and 17th centuries, the Mali Empire was enormously powerful, with a population of over 40 million people, a well-trained army and trade links with surrounding kingdoms. The city of Timbuktu was a centre of learning. Thousands of manuscripts have been preserved here, some dating back to the 1200s.

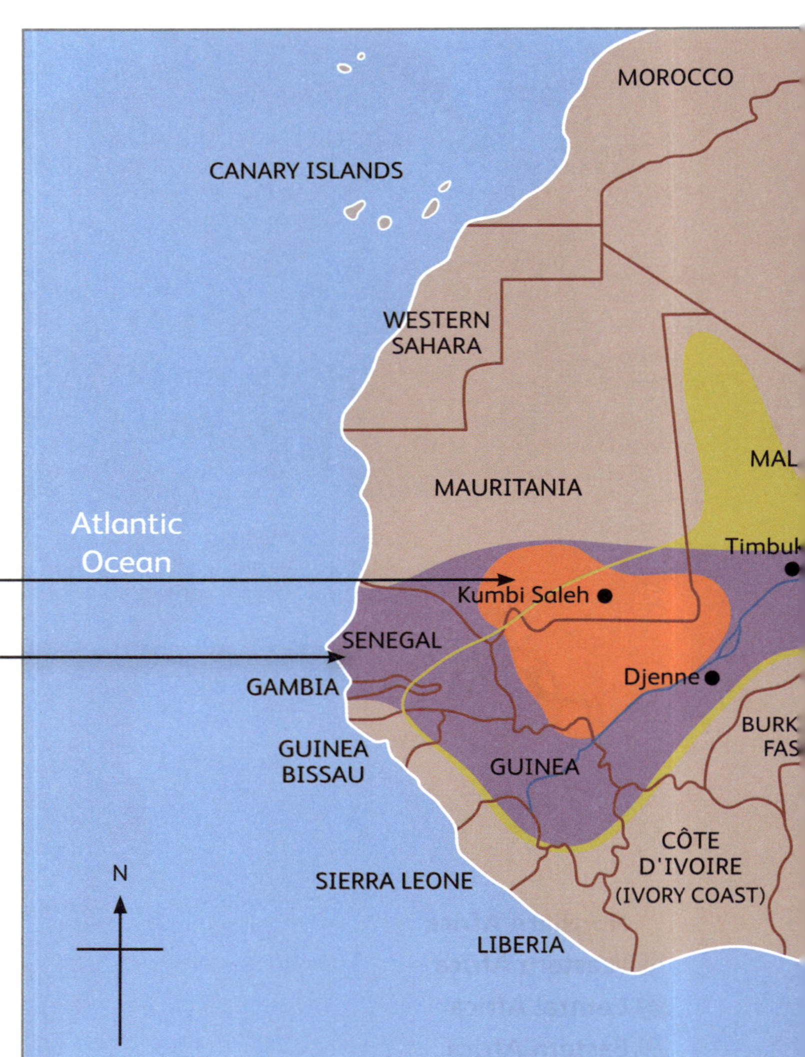

◀ **Bibliothèque des Manuscrits Al-Wangari is a library of ancient manuscripts in Timbuktu**

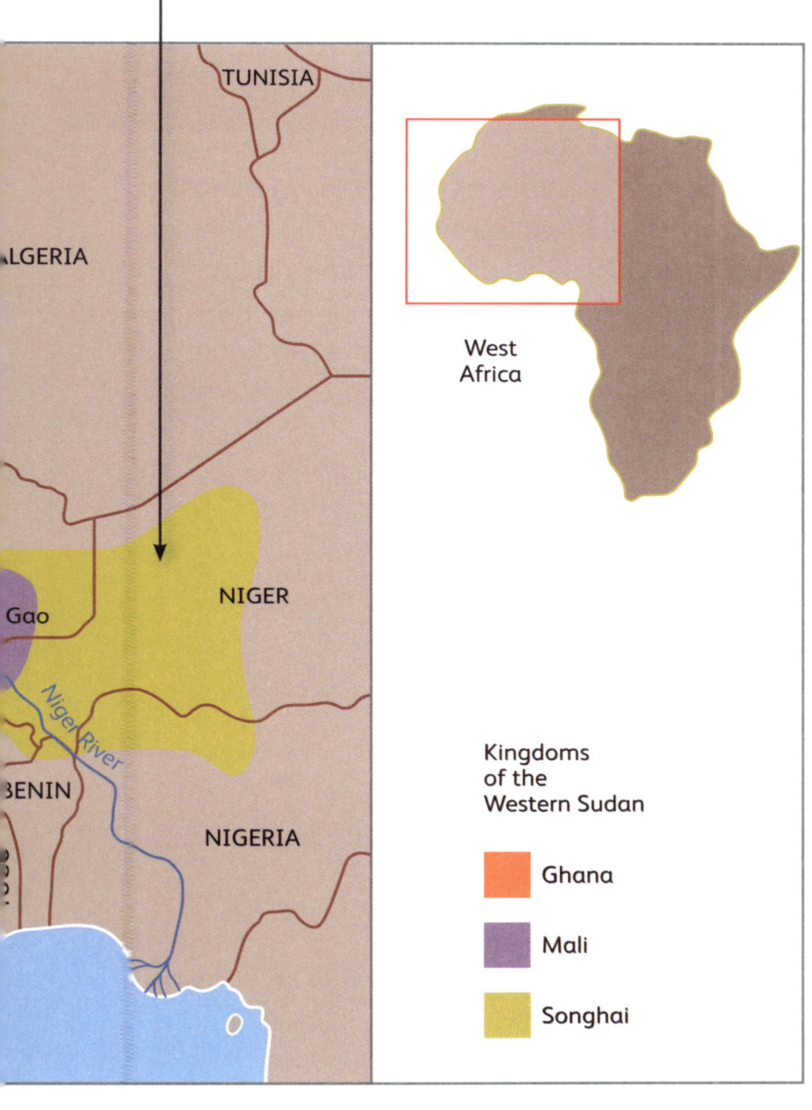

▲ The tomb of Askia Mohammed, the burial place of one of the rulers of the Songhai Empire from the 15th century

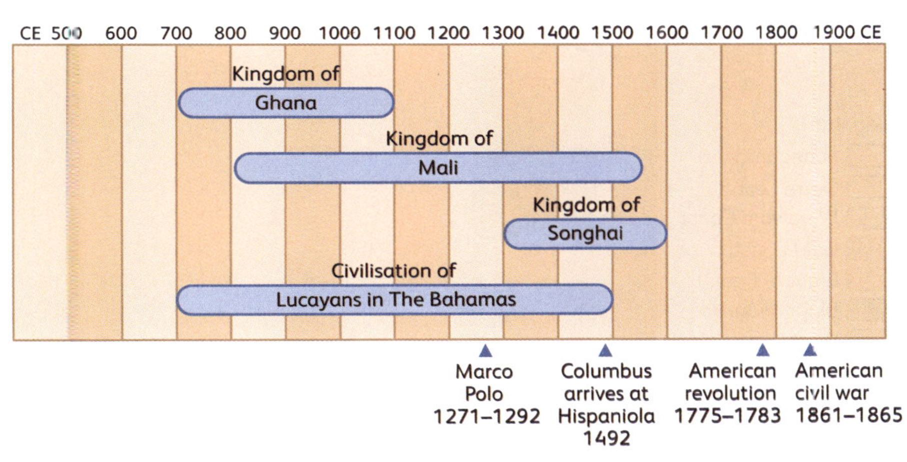

▲ **A bronze head sculpture from Ife**

The buildings of the Yoruba were mostly made from clay, a natural material that breaks down over time, so not many of these have survived. However, archaeologists have dug up more than 16,000 km of ancient walls used to defend the cities of this nation.

The Yoruba

The Yoruba lived in the areas today known as Nigeria, Benin and Togo. The city of Ife (or Ile-Ife) was the centre of the Yoruban culture, society and religion. Ife was founded around 500 CE and rose to great power by the 11th century. Later, the city was taken over by the Oyo Empire, a later kingdom of the Yoruba. The bronze art and sculpture of this kingdom were exceptionally skilful.

Activity 2 Research an African society

Our ancestors came from countries all along the west coast of Africa. European slave traders called these countries different names. These countries also have different names today.

Choose one of the empires or kingdoms you have read about, or research any other ancient African kingdom. You can do a short written or oral report. Include:

- the location
- important historical dates or events
- what made it famous or feared in the region
- beliefs or cultural practices of the time
- the names of some of the rulers
- what remains of it today.

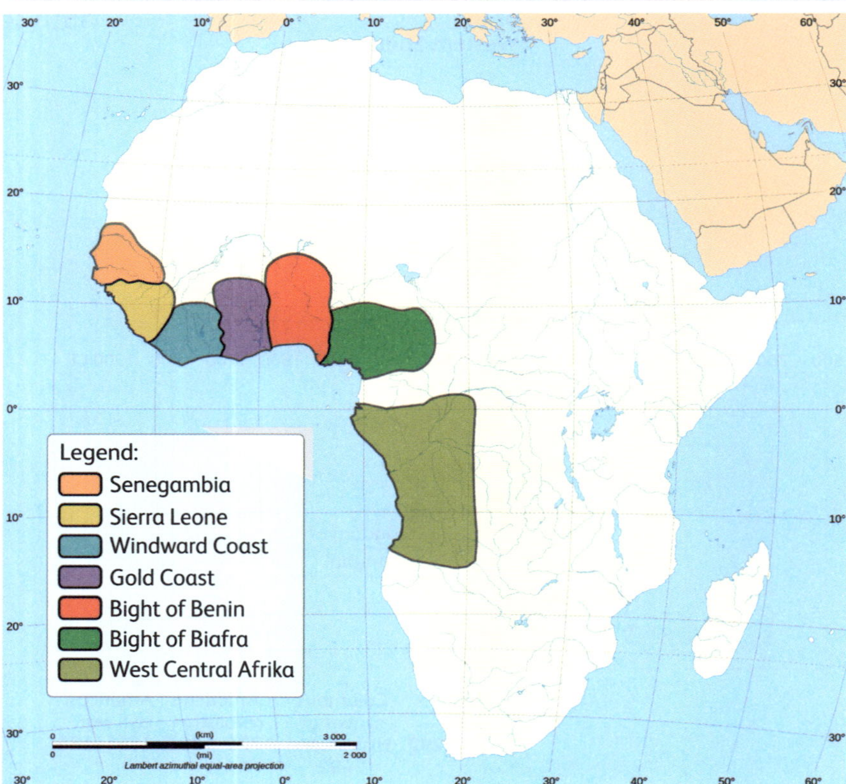

▶ **The regions from which enslaved people came**

The transatlantic slave trade

Slavery existed in many different forms in the ancient world. However, it had never been organised on such a massive scale, or with as much brutality as during the so-called Age of Discovery (or Age of Exploration). This was the period from the early 1500s, through the 1700s, when Europeans set sail to explore and conquer other lands. This period gave rise to one of the biggest industries of the early modern world: the **transatlantic slave trade**. It is sometimes called the **triangular slave trade** because it took place between three locations: Africa, the West Indies and America.

> **Word power**
>
> transatlantic slave trade
> triangular slave trade

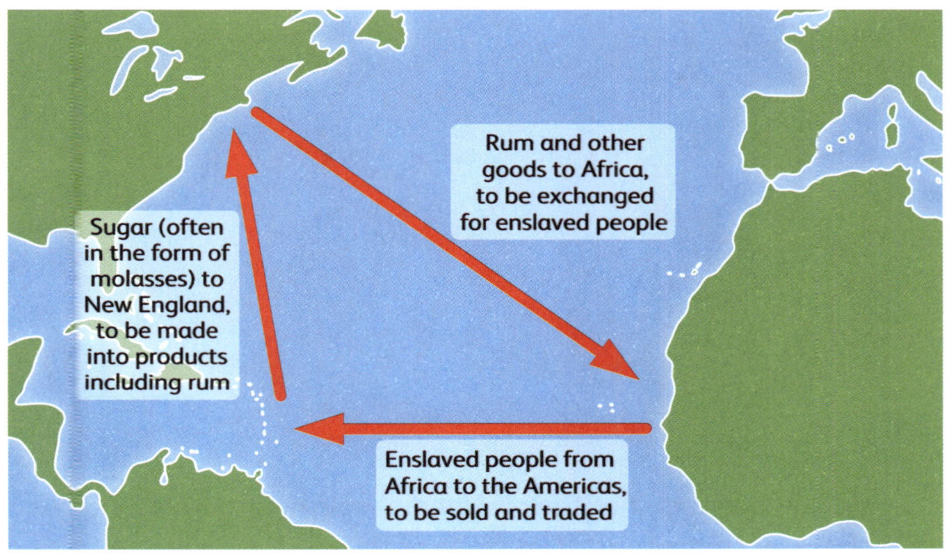

◄ The transatlantic slave trade was also known as the triangular slave trade.

Activity 3 Sequence events

1   In groups, discuss what you have learnt so far about the early people of The Bahamas.
2   Draw a flow chart, diagram or timeline ordering these events in sequence:

- American Revolution
- Slave ships bring captured West Africans to work on the plantations
- British colonise America
- Eleutherans leave The Bahamas after struggling to grow crops
- Loyalists flee America because they want to remain part of Britain
- Christopher Columbus sets sail from Spain to find a new route to China
- Columbus encounters the Taíno in the West Indies
- Enslavement and destruction of Lucayans and other Taíno
- Loyalists move to Bahamas with their enslaved people

The Middle Passage

European slave traders usually did not travel inland in Africa. Instead, they paid African middlemen in rum and other goods. These middlemen raided villages to kidnap people, who they then brought back to the coast to trade with the Europeans.

Chained or roped together, the captured people had to walk for days or weeks to reach the coast. This stage of their journey was the **First Passage**. Often they had no food or water. Many died along the way. Once at the coast, the captives would see a terrifying sight: the sea and the huge ships with their white European crew. They were packed into the ships like cargo. The ships were designed to fit as many people in as small a space as possible. Eventually, when the ship was ready to sail, the kidnapped Africans embarked on the journey known as the **Middle Passage**. This was the journey from Africa to the Americas.

This diagram shows how the captured people were packed into the ships. They had no room to move, no sanitation and no fresh water. They were usually fed twice a day, but many died from weakness, starvation, disease or malnutrition.

Word power

First Passage
Middle Passage

▶ **This illustration shows people being captured and sent into bondage**

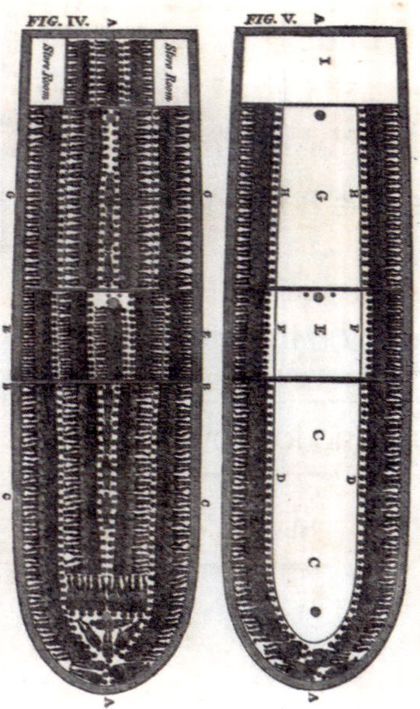

▲ **This drawing from 1791 shows a diagram used on slave ships as guidance for how to pack enslaved people**

Resistance on slave ships

Enslaved people did not go willingly into captivity. They resisted in a variety of ways.

Many committed suicide, either by refusing to eat or by jumping overboard. Enslaver crews used violent punishments to discourage this. They force-fed or tortured those who would not eat. People who jumped overboard might be shot or left to drown, or brought back on board and tortured as an example to others.

The enslaved people came from many different cultures, and did not share a language. They developed forms of singing and body percussion to communicate. This became one of the roots of call-and-response singing, which was also used to organise resistance.

There were many **uprisings** and mutinies. Sometimes rebels managed to kill some of the crew members. However, this usually resulted in punishments and killings to terrify the rest of the surviving enslaved people so that they would not do the same.

The Africans used religious **idols** and **fetishes** – objects they believed would have supernatural powers that could be used for harm or protection. They used incantations and curses to try and harm or scare their captors.

Word power

uprising
idol
fetish

▲ An illustration of a mutiny on a slave ship

Activity 4 The journey of the enslaved people

1   Trace a portion of the world map from your school atlas. Mark the journey that enslaved people from West Africa took to reach The Bahamas.
2   Write an essay, diary entry, poem or song about the story of the Middle Passage.

Cultural contributions of our African ancestors

Ships often stopped in Nassau on their way to America. The slave traders sold enslaved African captives to the Loyalists at slave **auctions**. For those enslaved people who survived the Middle Passage, they now faced a new chapter of hardship: forced labour and a life without freedom or rights on a plantation. However, the slave traders could not take away the cultural heritage that the enslaved people brought with them from their ancient civilisations in West Africa. Aspects of this rich heritage still forms part of our Bahamian identity and culture.

Activity 5 The impact of slavery

1 Draw a Venn diagram with two overlapping sets. Label the first set 'Our Bahamian culture' and the second set 'West African culture'. Work with a partner. Fill in your ideas to show how our culture today overlaps with that of our ancestors.

2 **a** As a class, discuss how an auction works. Make sure you understand these terms: auctioneer, price, bidder, bid.

   b Dramatise an auction for something like a pair of sneakers or a pack of football cards. The teacher can be the auctioneer and the students can be the bidders.

   c Discuss why we no longer buy and sell people in auctions. How can we ensure this never happens again?

Reflection

What feelings and emotions did you experience during this chapter? How does this period of our history make you feel?

Word power

continent
globe
country
compass rose
cardinal point

In this unit, you will:

- use a globe to identify continents and countries
- use map legends and keys
- identify the eight directional points of the compass
- draw and label a compass rose
- identify and use lines of longitude and latitude to locate places
- measure distances on a map using scale.

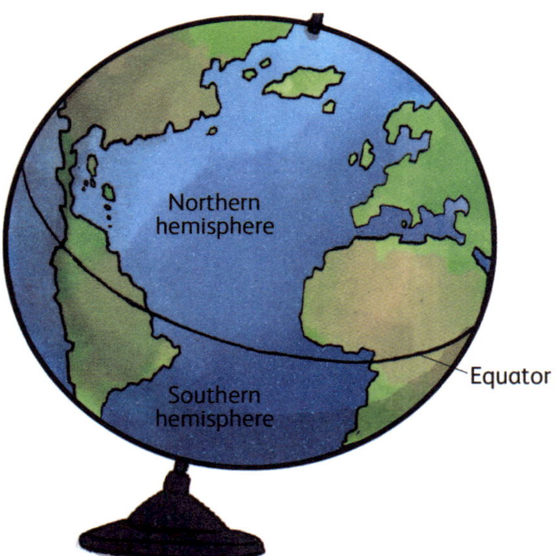

▲ A globe of the Earth

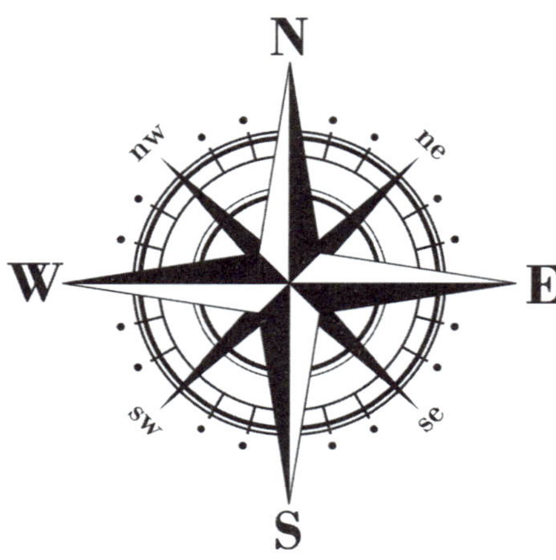

▲ A compass rose

Our location on Earth

Planet Earth is a ball shape called a geoid (meaning 'Earth shape'). Most of the Earth is covered in water. The land is divided into seven **continents**. In order from largest to smallest, they are Asia, Africa, North America, South America, Antarctica, Europe and Australia. Smaller islands are grouped with the nearest continent. When you look at a **globe**, you can see the shape and location of all the continents, as well as islands and seas. You can also locate each **country**.

A **compass rose** is a diagram that represents the four **cardinal points** – north (N), south (S), west (W) and east (E). They are also called compass directions.

Between those four main points are the intercardinal points – northwest (NW), northeast (NE), southwest (SW) and southeast (SE).

Activity 1 Where we are

Imagine that you are a scientist who has made contact with aliens in outer space. You need to send them directions to find your home in The Bahamas. Write directions. Include your planet, hemisphere, continent, country and town.

On a world map, you can see lines drawn across the map from one side to the other, and other lines from the top to the bottom. These lines form a **grid** over the map that we can use to locate positions. The horizontal lines are called **lines of latitude**, and the vertical lines are called **lines of longitude**. Lines of latitude and longitude only exist on maps. They do not exist in the real world.

The line of latitude that runs around the middle of the Earth is called the Equator. The Equator divides the Earth into the northern and southern **hemispheres**. The line of longitude that runs from north to south and passes through the town of Greenwich in the UK is known as the Prime Meridian or Greenwich Meridian. This line divides the Earth into western and eastern hemispheres.

> **Word power**
>
> grid
> line of latitude
> line of longitude
> hemisphere
> cartographer

Activity 2 Locating places on the world map

Use your school atlas.

1 Identify two continents that have the Equator running through them.

2 Is The Bahamas in the northern or southern hemisphere? Explain how you can work this out.

3 Look up the section in your atlas that shows lines of latitude. Identify:

   a two lines of latitude north of the Equator

   b two lines of latitude south of the Equator.

4 Identify four countries that are south of The Bahamas and west of Puerto Rico.

5 Look carefully at a map of the Caribbean region. Identify islands that have the Tropic of Cancer running through them.

6

> People who draw maps are called **cartographers**. In olden times, they would use decorative compass roses to beautify their maps. Sometimes they used heraldry, the symbolic form of design used in Coats of Arms and national crests.

▲ **Decorative compass rose designs**

Using what you have learnt about national symbols, our Bahamian history, and the elements of a compass rose, do your own compass rose design. Let it show your Bahamian history and heritage.

Political and physical maps

The Bahamas is an **archipelago**: a collection of small islands. There are more than 700 small islands in our country. Many of our neighbouring countries are also islands, or groups of islands.

A country is a political territory that identifies as a nation. People from that country share a nationality, and each country has its own leaders and laws. The **border** marks the edges of the country. In the Caribbean, most of our countries are islands, so the **coastline** usually determines the border. In other countries, the border may follow a river or mountain range, or simply a line on a map which people have agreed on as the border. Human-made borders often look like straight lines on the map.

Political maps only show country borders, and locations of cities and capital cities. Some may also show regional boundaries such as parishes. **Physical maps** include information about geographical features such as rivers, lakes, mountains and forests.

Word power

archipelago
border
coastline
political map
physical map

Did you know?

'Archipelago' comes from the Greek 'arkhi' meaning chief and 'pelagos' meaning pool or sea. Originally this was the name for the Aegean Sea, which had many small islands. Later the term came to mean any collection of islands.

▲ **This is a physical map of Mexico**

Activity 3 Political and physical maps

1 Discuss with a friend how colours are used on the physical map of Mexico. What do you think each of these shows:

   a the blue lines   **b** the larger blue areas

   c the green areas   **d** the light brown areas

   e the darker brown areas   **f** the red dots

   g the red square?

2 Look at the political map of Africa below.

   a Name three African countries that are islands in the sea around the main continent of Africa.

   b Name three countries on the east coast of Africa.

   c Identify a country that has seven or more neighbouring countries along its borders. List the names of the neighbouring countries. Get a partner to guess the name of the country you identified.

▲ **This is a political map of Africa**

Using scale

Have you ever zoomed out on an app or website like Google Maps, to make places look smaller and smaller? Or perhaps you have been in an airplane and seen how you can see all the places on the ground get smaller and smaller as you go further up?

This can help you to understand what we mean when we say that maps are drawn to scale. A map is like an accurately zoomed-out picture of a place on Earth. Look at the map below. It has a **scale** of 1 cm to 100 km. That means that 1 cm on the map represents 100 km in real life.

There are different ways we can show scale:

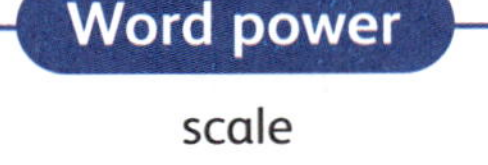

Word power

scale

- 1 cm : 100 km — This scale says that 1 cm on the map is equal to 100 km on the ground.

- This is a line scale. It also tells us that 1 cm on the map is equal to 100 km (or 62 miles) on the ground.

▲ The Bahamas

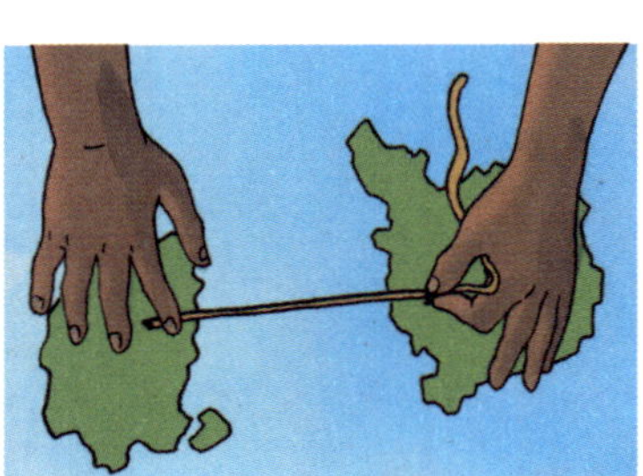

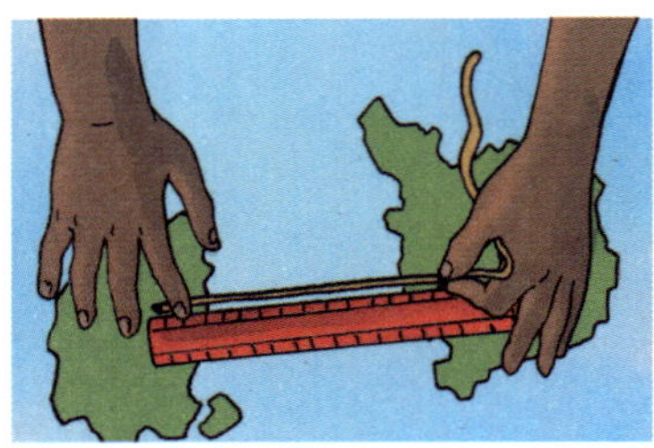

▲ Measuring scale

When you want to measure the distance between two places on a map, you use a ruler. If the route you want to measure is curved, first follow the route with a piece of string, then measure that against your ruler. Use the scale to calculate the real distance. For example, on this map, the distance from San Salvador to Samana Cay is 13 mm or 1.3 cm. We know that 1 cm = 100 km on this map.
1.3 × 100 = 130 so the distance between these two places is about 130 km in real life.

Activity 4 Use a scale map

1 In which direction must you travel to get from:
   a Greendale to Redroad?
   b Golden Bay to Redroad?
2 Which village is located furthest towards the north of the island?
3 Which of the compass points would you use to describe the location of Sea View on the island?
4 What is the scale of this map? Complete the sentence:
   _____ cm on the map = _____ km in real life.
5 Calculate the distance in real life from:
   a Redroad to Greendale
   b Golden Bay to Redroad
   c Glenpond to Golden Bay via Sea View.
6 Use string and a ruler to help you calculate the distance by road from Mount Catherine to Glenpond.

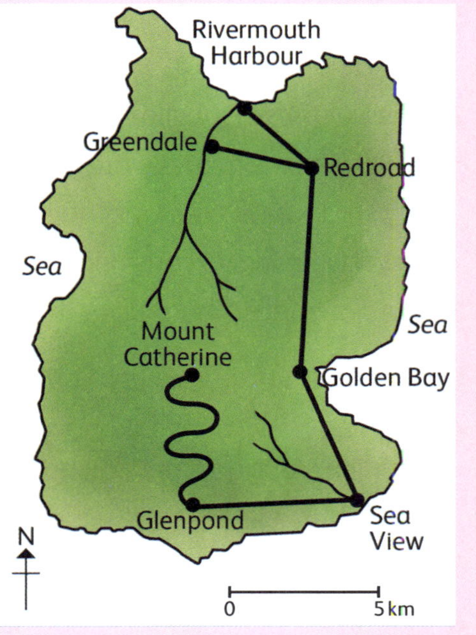

Activity 5 Create a scaled map

You will need:
- your atlas
- some graph paper (grid paper)
- a pencil
- a ruler

Use your atlas. Choose one of the islands in The Bahamas. You will create a scaled map or model of this island.

1 First trace the island using grid paper.
2 Next, decide by how much you are going to scale up your map.
3 Copy the traced island, using a larger square size for each square on your original map.
4 Now calculate the scale of your new map.

Tips

For an extra creative challenge, create a scaled 3-D model of one of the islands. You can use card, clay or any other materials.

Reflection

Why do you think reading maps is an important skill? How has technology changed the way we find and read maps?

Theme 1 What have you learnt?

Unit 1 National pride and patriotism

1 Write a sentence explaining each term:
   a patriotism   **b** national pride.

2 Answer these questions about the Coat of Arms.
   a Which two animals are shown on the Coat of Arms?
   b Which other elements have the same colours as each of the animals?
   c Which event is commemorated by the ship?

3 The national anthem uses a slightly different name for The Bahamas. What name does it use?

Unit 2 The Lucayans and the arrival of Columbus

4 Imagine how you would have lived as a Lucayan before Columbus's arrival. Describe a day in your life. Your description should tell the reader a bit about the main activities of the Lucayans, what they ate and where they lived.

5 List three words that we still use today that come from the Lucayans.

6 The arrival of the Spanish had several negative outcomes for the Lucayans. Describe three of these.

Unit 3 The Eleutheran Adventurers

7 Explain what you understand by the term 'religious freedom' and why this was an important reason for the arrival of the Eleutheran Adventurers.

Unit 4 The Loyalists

8 What was the main difference between the Loyalists and the Eleutherans?

9 Look at this example of a Loyalist house. List any four features it has that make it typical of the Loyalist style.

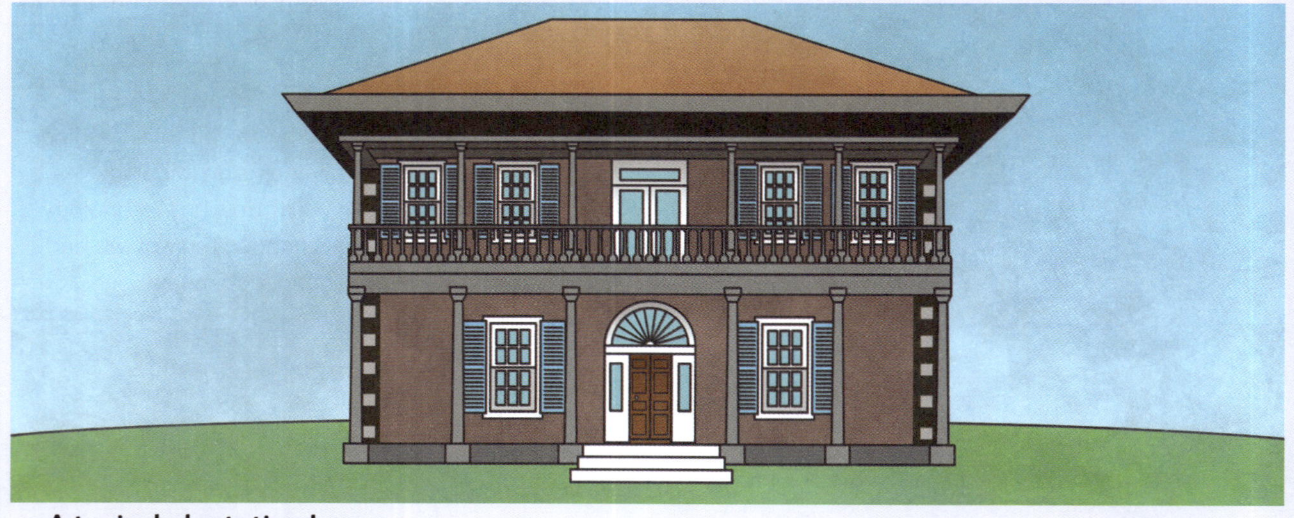

▲ **A typical plantation house**

(Continued)

Unit 5 Our African ancestors

10 Name any five countries from central or western Africa that would have been the homes of many Bahamians' ancestors.

11 Why was the transatlantic slave trade also known as the triangular slave trade? Draw a diagram to support your answer.

12 Draw a flow diagram describing some of the things that might happen to an African person before, during and after going on the Middle Passage.

13 Enslaved African people brought many cultural contributions to The Bahamas. Identify one which you feel is most significant for you. Write a few sentences describing this tradition and why it is important for you.

Unit 6 Using maps

14 Write the labels that are missing from the map:

a the name of this island

b a line of longitude

c the name of this island

d a line of latitude

e the name of the capital situated here

f the name of this ocean.

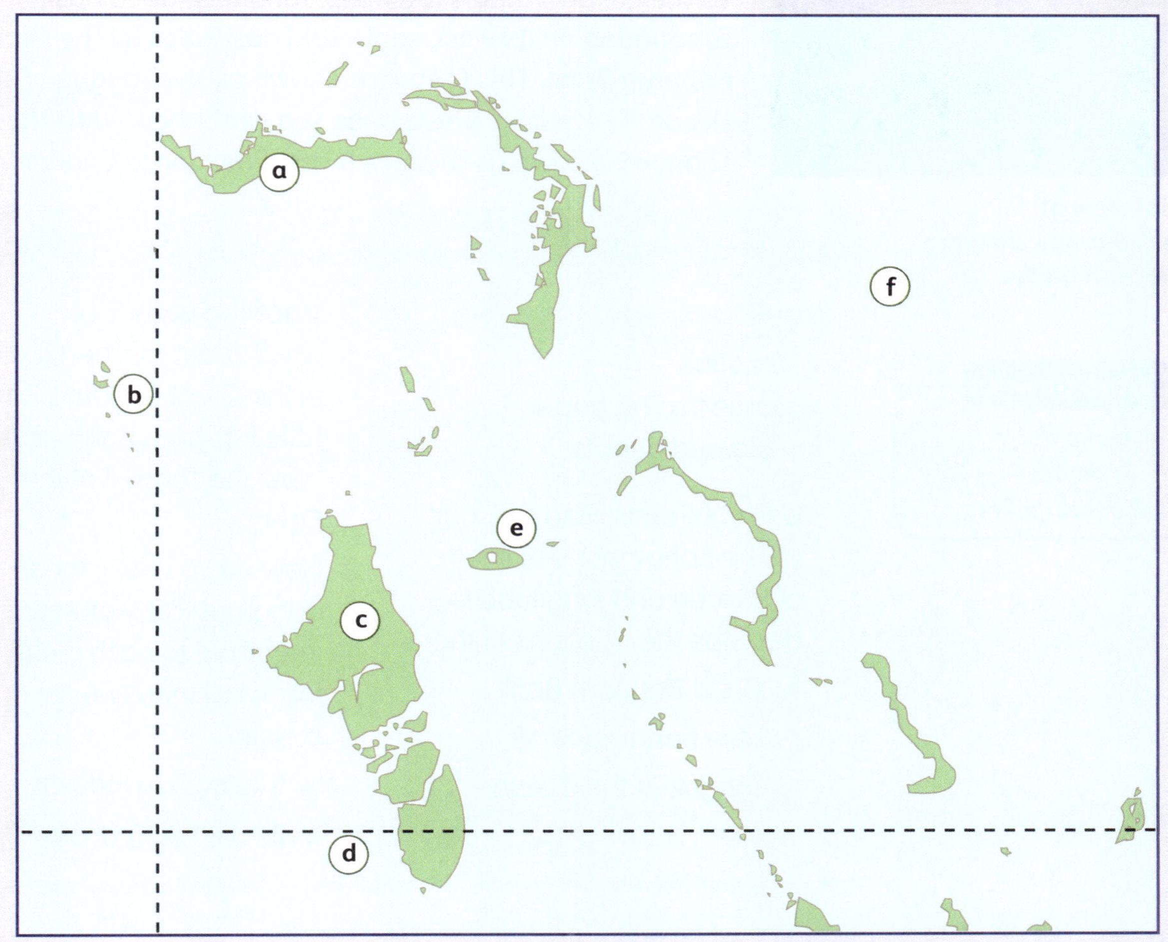

> **In this unit, you will:**
> - discuss the significance of the Little and Great Bahama Banks
> - locate and compare different islands within The Bahamas
> - distinguish between climate and weather.

▲ Aerial view of The Bahamas showing the ocean banks

Word power

aerial view
banks
carbonate deposit

The Little and Great Bahama Banks

This is an **aerial view** of The Bahamas. The light turquoise shapes are **banks** within the deeper ocean. The larger G-shaped formation is the Great Bahama Bank. The smaller formation to the north is the Little Bahama Bank.

Ocean banks are platforms around our islands where the water is much shallower than the surrounding ocean. These banks are made of **carbonate deposits** formed over thousands of years, mostly from crushed shells.

To the east of Andros is a deep, tongue-shaped basin surrounded on its west, south and east sides by the Great Bahama Bank. This feature is known as the Tongue of the Ocean. The region where deep sea water flows into the Tongue is known as the Northwest Providence Channel.

Activity 1 Locating the Great and Little Banks

You will need:
- an atlas
- some tracing paper
- coloured pencils

1 Use your atlas. Find the map of The Bahamas. Use lines of latitude and longitude to describe the positions of the:
   - **a** Great Bahama Bank
   - **b** Little Bahama Bank
   - **c** Tongue of the Ocean

2 Trace the islands of The Bahamas. Then shade in the Great Bahama Bank, Little Bahama Bank, and label the Tongue of the Ocean.

3 How do you think these geographical features are important to each of the following industries in our country:
   - **a** the tourism industry
   - **b** the fishing industry?

The Banks are a very important part of our marine life. The Great Bank has one of the largest **barrier reefs** on Earth, which extends for around 225 km. If your atlas has a section about fishing, you will notice that the banks form the main fishing areas of The Bahamas. This is because the banks provide a rich habitat for many fish and crustaceans. The shallow waters of the banks also provide many tourist attractions, such as scuba diving, fishing, snorkelling and swimming.

Word power

barrier reef

▲ This map shows the locations of cays and islands in relation to the banks

Activity 2 Tourist attractions

1 Discuss with your group what tourist activities take place on the Little and Great Bahama Banks. If possible, visit a local tourist information centre and get some brochures about activities for tourists.

2 In groups, make up a radio or TV advertisement talking about activities that visitors might enjoy.

Our many islands

The Bahamas is made up of nearly 700 islands, but most of them are not inhabited by people. This table gives some information about ten of our biggest islands. In addition to these islands, people also live on Berry Islands, Bimini, Crooked Island, Harbour Island, Mayaguana, Ragged Island, Rum Cay and San Salvador.

The southern islands of The Bahamas receive less rainfall than the other islands. As a result, less vegetation grows there. Farming is more difficult and there are fewer natural resources for people to use to make a living.

ISLANDS	Abaco	Acklins	Andros	Cat Island
What is its crest?				
What was the total population in 2010?	16,025	560	7,242	1,503
What is its size in km²?	1,681 km²	497 km²	5,959 km²	389 km²
What is its highest point in yd?	41 yd	47 yd	39 yd	69 yd
Which are its main towns?	Cooper's Town March Harbour Sandy Point	Spring Point	Nicholl's Town Fresh Creek Kemp's Bay	Arthur's Town New Bight Port Howe
What are some of its products?	Fish Vegetables	Cascarilla bark	Vegetables Citrus fruits Water Manufactured goods	Vegetables
Which places do tourists like to visit as well as the main towns?	Treasure Cay Hope Town Man of War Cay Green Turtle Cay	Castle Island lighthouse	Androsia factory Blue holes	Caves Mt Alvernia

Tips

You can use mnemonics to help you in many different school subjects. For example, in Maths, you may have learnt mnemonics to help you remember the metric units of measure, and the order of operations. Can you think of them?

Activity 3 Know your islands

1 Use your atlas to answer the questions.

   a Which two of the five southern islands are listed in the table above?

2 Name the remaining three southern islands, and list at least one town or village on each.

3 A mnemonic is a way of using words or letters to remember something, for example through a sentence or rhyme. Work with a partner to make up your own mnemonics to remember the names of the islands in the table from most northerly to most southerly.

◀ A pineapple plantation on Eleuthera

Eleuthera and Spanish Wells	Exuma	Grand Bahama	The Inaguas	Long Island	New Providence
7,726	7,314	51,756	911	3,024	248,948
518 km²	290 km²	1,373 km²	1,679 km²	596 km²	207 km²
63 yd	42 yd	23 yd	36 yd	59 yd	42 yd
Spanish Wells Dunmore Town Governor's Harbour Rock Sound	George Town	West End Eight Mile Rock Freeport City	Matthew Town	Deadmans Cay Clarence Town Stella Maris	Nassau
Pineapples Vegetables Citrus fuits Fish	Onions	Medicines Petroleum products Chemicals	Salt Cascarilla bark	Livestock Fish Citrus fruits	Alcoholic beverages Livestock
Glass Window Preacher's Cave Pink sand beaches	Elizabeth Harbour National Land-Sea Park Plantation ruins	Garden of the Groves Lucayan National Park	Morton's Salt Company National Park Flamingos	Dean's Blue Hole caves Columbus monument	Bay Street Forts Queen's Staircase Straw market Water tower

Activity 4 Compare and contrast

Choose one of the southern islands and one of the central or northwest islands. List the differences you notice in size, population and products.

▶ A fish stand on Crooked Island

Our climate and weather

When we talk about **weather**, we are talking about the conditions of the atmosphere – the air and sky around us. If you read or listen to a weather report, you may hear the forecaster discussing several aspects of weather, including:

- **temperature** – how hot or cold the air is, measured in degrees Celsius or degrees Fahrenheit
- **precipitation** – such as rain, snow or hail
- **atmospheric pressure** – the weight of the atmosphere overhead
- **wind** – how fast the air is moving, and in which direction
- **humidity** – the amount of water vapour in the air
- **cloud formations** – for example whether the sky is overcast or clear.

Weather conditions change from day to day, but for each place, weather usually follows certain patterns that we call the **climate** of that place. For example, The Bahamas has a warm, sunny climate, with temperatures between 26 °C and 32 °C in summer. Even in winter it does not get much colder than about 16 °C. **Meteorologists** (people who study the weather) call this a sub-tropical climate.

Word power

weather
precipitation
atmospheric pressure
humidity
climate
meteorologist

Reflection

If you were speaking to someone who lives in another country, how would you describe the weather of The Bahamas?

Activity 5 Weather instruments

1 Match each of the following instruments to one of the aspects of weather you have read about. Discuss with your group how you think it works.

▶ windsock   ▶ rain gauge   ▶ thermometer

2 This table shows monthly average temperatures in Nassau. Use this data to answer the questions.

	Jan	Feb	Mar	Apr	May	Jun	Jul	Aug	Sep	Oct	Nov	Dec
°C	21	21	22	23	25	27	28	28	27	26	23	22
°F	69.8	69.8	71.6	73.4	77	80.6	82.4	82.4	80.6	78.8	73.4	71.6

a Identify the two coldest months.   b Identify the two warmest months.

c Which are our summer months?   d Which are our winter months?

3 Identify a place in your atlas that you think has a climate very different to ours.

Do research about that place and report back on the seasons and climate there.

8 Natural resources and food production

In this unit, you will:

- identify natural resources of The Bahamas
- describe sustainable ways to harvest natural resources
- list foods that we produce and manufacture in The Bahamas
- connect specific islands with the foods they produce
- describe the process of bottling and canning
- list jobs directly and indirectly created by your island's resources.

What are natural resources?

All living things need air, water and sunlight to survive. Plants need soil in which to grow, and we need plants in order to produce our own food, and to feed livestock such as poultry, goats, pigs and cattle. A **resource** is a raw material or a supply that we use to meet our needs. Air, water, sunlight, soil and plants and animals are **natural resources**. We use these natural resources to make different products. Here are some examples of natural resources.

Word power
resource
natural resources

Activity 1 Defining natural resources

1. Which of the following are not natural resources?

   fish and shellfish • plates • sand • rocks

   windows • books • wood • paint • petroleum

   diamonds • cotton • plastic • wool • eggs

2. Discuss your answers to Question 1. Use them to help you develop a definition for what is and is not a natural resource.

Activity 2 Collect examples of natural resources

As a class, make a display for your classroom showing the different types of resources found in The Bahamas. Discuss how you can show each resource. It may be possible to have samples of some resources (such as water, soil, air) in jars. Other resources may require you to make drawings or models.

▲ Natural resources are resources we use from nature, such as fuels, solar and wind energy, water, wood, arable land and livestock

Using resources sustainably

We rely on our natural resources from our environment for food, and to earn a living. Our islands are surrounded by the sea, with rich marine resources. In the past, people harvested sponge from the sea. Sisal was another important resource. Each natural resource forms an important part of our lives on Earth. This picture shows some uses of a common resource – sand.

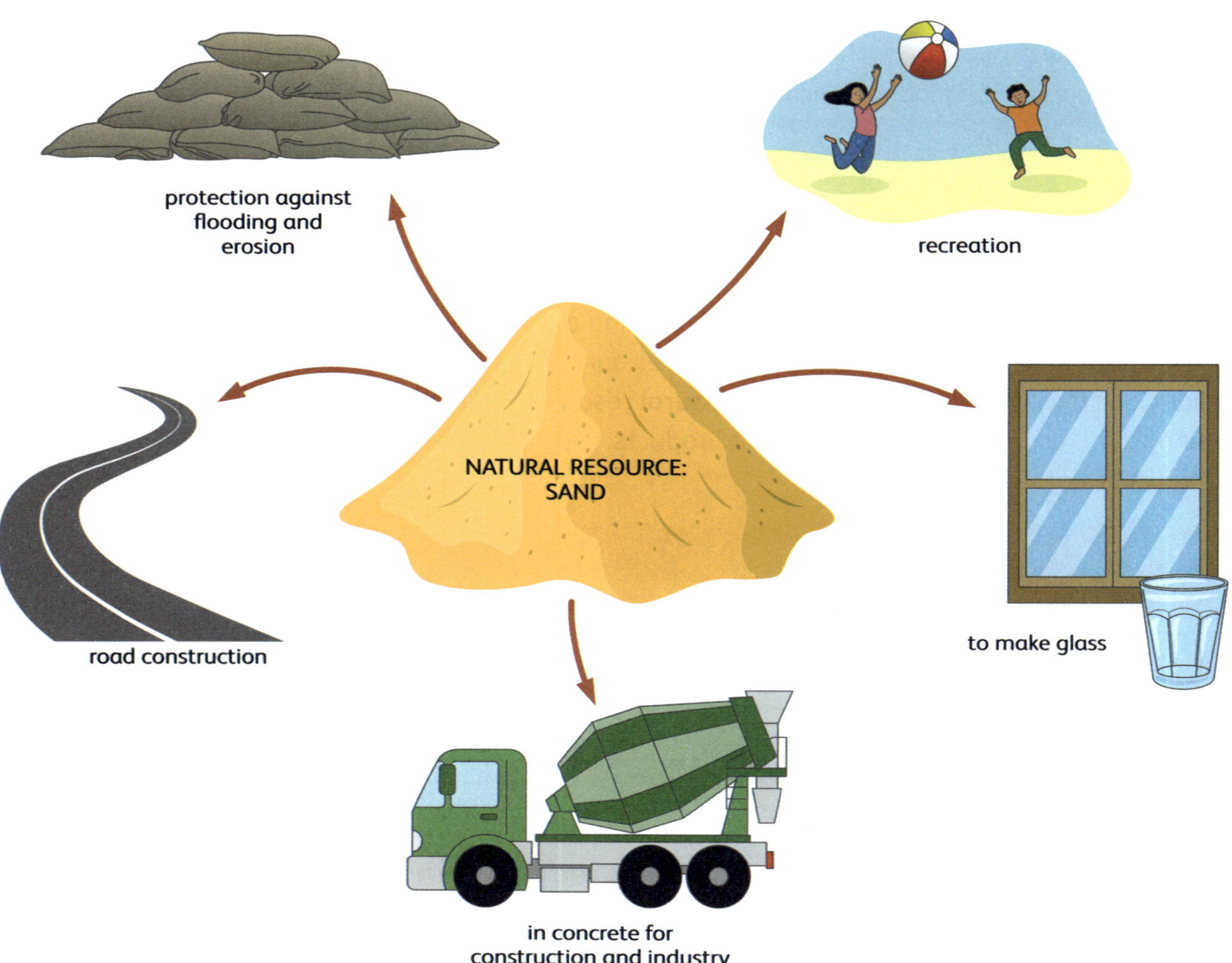

Activity 3 Link resources to your life

1 Think about the importance of marine life in The Bahamas.

   a Draw a spider diagram showing the many ways that people use this natural resource.

   b Write a short paragraph about what would happen if this resource was no longer available.

2 Repeat **1a** and **b** for another natural resource of your own choice.

Picking ripe crops is called **harvesting**. To harvest a resource also means to take it from the environment and use it. We use other resources too. For example: we catch fish, collect other resources from the sea, and extract different types of rocks and earth from mines and quarries. We also use energy – solar energy from sunshine, wind energy from moving air, and hydroelectric power from dams and lakes. How we harvest a resource depends on where it occurs in the environment, and its particular properties.

Some resources are **finite**. There is a fixed amount in the environment, and eventually they will run out. **Minerals** such as gold, coal, copper, diamonds and bauxite are all finite resources. Mining is the process of taking these resources from the earth.

Word power

harvesting
finite
mineral
renewable
semi-renewable
sustainable

▲ Minerals in the earth are a finite resource

▲ Wind energy is a renewable resource

Renewable resources can grow back or increase again in supply. For example, wind energy is a natural resource that we can use to produce electric power. People use wind turbines to harness this energy. As the huge blades turn, they activate a generator that produces electricity. Wind is a renewable resource. No matter how much we use, there is more available.

Resources like soil and water are **semi-renewable**. They stay healthy if we use them in a **sustainable** way. Unsustainable farming practices deplete the soil. Others replenish the nutrients and make it possible to keep growing crops for many generations.

▲ A papaya farm

Activity 4 How we harvest different resources

1 As a class, discuss the following natural resources. Do research if you need to.

salt cascarilla bark shrimp

2 Answer these questions for each resource:
   a Where is it found?
   b Does it grow or does it occur in the environment?
   c What do we use it for?
   d What is the process used to harvest it? Describe any special equipment we need to harvest it.
   e If we take it out of the environment, can it grow back or be replaced?
   f What kind of practices can protect this resource?

Aragonite mining in The Bahamas

Aragonite, also known as ooid sand, is a type of mineral found in The Bahamas. Normal sand forms from the broken-down shells of sea life. Aragonite forms the opposite way — it gradually builds up very slowly as dissolved minerals in the seawater precipitate into solid form. We export aragonite as a raw material because many countries use it in their cement and concrete production. However, in 2020, the Minister of the Environment spoke out against aragonite mining.

Connections

▲ **This is what the Minister of the Environment said about aragonite in 2020**

Activity 5 For or against?

1 Write in your own words the arguments for and against aragonite mining in The Bahamas.

2 Say which view you think is more convincing, and why.

Food production

Because of our warm climate and sandy soil, only some crops grow well in The Bahamas. Most farming takes place in the Abacos. We farm tropical fruits such as avocado, pineapple, banana and papaya. We also farm melons, and citrus fruits such as grapefruit, oranges and limes. Many farmers focus on poultry, producing eggs and poultry meat. Others keep livestock for dairy or meat farming.

Fruits, vegetables, milk, meat and eggs are raw materials that we can use in food production. Think about a lemon. Some lemons will be sold in fresh form, but many will become ingredients in other food products.

▲ Lemons are used in many products

Connections

Remember our Lucayan ancestors? They survived in this environment by fishing.

Remember the Eleutherans? They tried farming, and nearly starved.

Activity 6 Home-grown food products

Work in groups for this activity.

1 Arrange to go to a grocery store or supermarket together.

2 Find examples of local products. They should say 'made in Bahamas' or 'product of Bahamas' on the label. Find at least two examples in each category and draw up your own table like the one below.

3 For each product, write the details of the manufacturer. If possible, include the island where they make the product.

Food products made mainly from:				
Fruits	Vegetables	Meats	Dairy	Other

Bottling and canning food

Fresh foods begin to spoil or decay after harvesting. Since ancient times, people have found ways to **preserve** food – to slow down the rate of **spoilage** and make it last longer. You may hear this called 'extending the **shelf life**'. In ancient times, people mostly used salt to preserve food. They would salt meats to make them last longer, and pickle vegetables in brine (salty water). The invention of refrigeration in the 20th century made it possible to keep food cold, which keeps it fresh for longer. We can also freeze foods.

In The Bahamas, we have many companies and home industries that use **bottling** and **canning** as methods of preserving food. You can read about this process in the cartoon strip.

Word power

preserve
spoilage
shelf life
bottling
canning
perishable

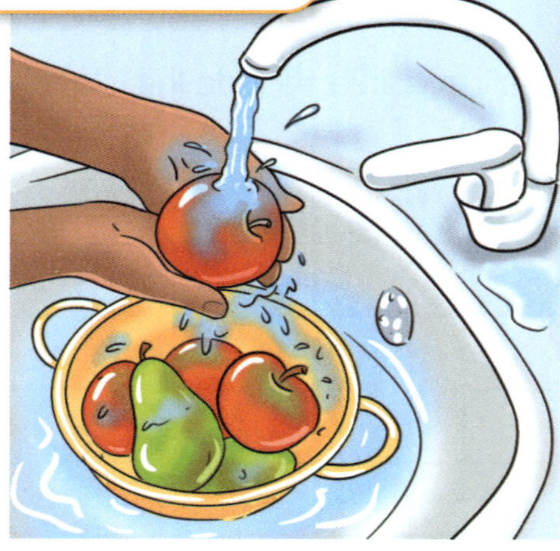

Activity 7 Bottling and canning

1 List five foods that you use at home (or that you have seen in the store) that are sold in cans.

2 List five foods that are sold in bottles.

3 Find out the meanings of the following terms used in canning and bottling:

   a hot-packing   b sealing   c headroom

   d pressure canning   e water bath.

4 Research the process for bottling one of the following foods, or another food of your choice: home-cooked tomato sauce, fresh chillis or prepared hot sauce, jam or jelly, pineapple slices. Draw a flow diagram showing the main steps in the process.

Natural resources create jobs

Wherever people live, they need to earn a living. Having a job allows people to earn money, which they use to meet many different needs. The natural resources in a country provide many different jobs. Some natural resources provide jobs directly. For example, our islands have large, flat areas of land, with soil and a tropical climate that we can use for agriculture (farming). Farmers get their work directly from this resource. Other jobs are created indirectly, for example:

▲ The farmer needs farm equipment. Someone might set up a business to import and supply tractors, hardware and fertiliser

▲ Drivers and delivery personnel transport the goods from the farm to customers, and to the ports for export

▲ Agricultural scientists conduct research and experiments to study agriculture. They may test the plants for diseases, test the soil, study productivity and yields, and also help develop new strains of plants

▲ Agricultural engineers help to design farm equipment and facilities. They help farmers ensure a steady supply of power and water. They may also help avoid pollution and environmental damage

Activity 8 Jobs indirectly created by natural resources

1 Look at each job. Discuss with a partner how natural resources might help create opportunities for this kind of job.

graphic designer · banker · civil servant · labourer · plumber · cook

builder · receptionist · entrepreneur · software developer · photographer

2 Talk about the jobs that people in your family have. How are they related to natural resources found in The Bahamas?

9 Tourism

In this unit, you will:
- identify different types of visitors to The Bahamas
- analyse the value of tourism to our country
- discuss the role of Sir Stafford Sands in our tourism industry
- identify people who work in tourism.

What is tourism?

Tourists are people who travel to a place to visit it. Some tourists stop over for a few days, weeks or even months. People who spend one night or more are called **stopover visitors**. They use accommodation and other services. Most tourists come for a holiday, to enjoy our warm weather and beaches. We may categorise tourists in different ways, for example:

- Domestic tourists travel within their own country or region.
- International tourists come from other countries.
- Leisure tourists come on vacation, which may include a cruise or resort.
- Some tourists come to visit friends and relatives (VFR).
- Medical and health tourists travel for healthcare or wellness.
- Eco-tourists travel to experience nature.
- Cultural tourists come for events such as Junkanoo or festivals.
- Business tourists travel for work, for example to attend a convention.

Some of these categories overlap, for example a domestic tourist may be a business or leisure tourist.

▲ Cruise ships bring thousands of visitors to The Bahamas

Word power

tourist
stopover visitor

Tips

Remember, a percentage is a fraction out of 100. You need to convert your percentages to fractions out of 360 in order to work out each angle in the pie chart.

Activity 1 Where our tourists come from

1. Stopover tourists in The Bahamas come from different places. In 2022, we had 561,651 stopover visitors: 89% came from the USA, 4% from Canada, 3.8% from Europe, 1.4% from Latin America, 0.8% from the Caribbean, and 1% from other countries. Use this information to draw a pie chart.

2. Around three-quarters of our visitors are on vacation. List three other reasons people might visit The Bahamas.

3. Explain the difference between domestic and international tourism.

4. European tourists tend to spend more nights in The Bahamas than American tourists. Suggest a possible reason for this.

The history of tourism in The Bahamas

The tourism industry arose in the early 1800s with the development of new forms of transportation designed for comfortable travel. You will learn more about transport in Unit 4.

The early days – 1800s

▲ **Steamship from the Cunard Line**

In the 1800s, the idea of traveling for vacation or leisure gradually gained popularity in Europe and the USA. The Bahamian government passed several acts to try encourage visitors to the country: the Tourism Encouragement Act of 1851, and further Acts in 1854 and 1857. The 1857 Act allowed the Government to buy land for a grand hotel.

In 1859, the Government came to an agreement with a famous steamship company called the Cunard Line, and set up a regular steamship service to The Bahamas.

More hotels opened after that, and additional steamship services too.

Early 20th century developments

In 1914, the government set up the Tourism Development Board to promote The Bahamas as a tourist destination. However, World War I (1914–1918) slowed down tourism from the USA. In 1919, after the war ended, a seaplane service started offering transport between Florida and the islands.

▲ **Colonial Hotel, Nassau, in the 1920s**

In the 1920s, the tourist industry grew. Many new hotels sprang up. This was the time of Prohibition, when alcohol was banned in the USA. Americans travelled to The Bahamas for the locally produced rum. However, at the end of the 1920s, the Great Depression began in America. It was a time of terrible poverty and few people could afford to travel to the Caribbean.

Between the 1800s and the 1940s, the same challenge kept arising: as soon as tourism started to grow, it stopped again. The business was seasonal. Tourists came between November and February, when they wanted to get away from the cold weather at home, and stayed away for the rest of the year. The government decided that The Bahamas needed a more stable tourist industry that could continue all year round.

Boosts to tourism in the mid-20th century

Sir Stafford Sands is known as the 'Father of Tourism' in The Bahamas. He was a lawyer who later became the Minister of Finance. He also led the Tourism Development Board, which later became the Ministry of Tourism. He believed that the tourist industry was the key to economic prosperity for Bahamians. He was especially interested in attracting wealthy celebrities to The Bahamas. In the 1950s, he was responsible for developing the tourist industry by:

- supporting the building of large hotels
- campaigning for the legalisation of gambling
- encouraging the building of casinos in Nassau, New Providence and Freeport, Grand Bahama
- introducing air conditioning to the hotels
- setting up summer events such as parades, concerts and music festivals
- carrying out big advertising and marketing campaigns in the USA, Canada and Europe to attract tourists to The Bahamas.

▲ A portrait of Sir Stafford Sands as he used to appear on a Bahamian banknote

America imposed a trade embargo on Cuba in 1961, after Fidel Castro's coup in that country. Before the coup, Cuba was a popular destination for American tourists. After the embargo, many Americans travelled to The Bahamas instead. By 1968, The Bahamas had 1 million visitors in a single year.

This table shows the changes in arrivals to Grand Bahama between 1963 and 1968:

Tourist arrivals 1963–1968			
Year	**By Air**	**By Sea**	**Total**
1963	23,000	3,000	26,000
1964	89,000	20,000	109,000
1965	127,769	68,231	196,000
1966	155,456	48,714	204,170
1967	229,635	23,500	253,135
1968	295,117	36,909	332,026

Shifts in tourism in the 1970s and 1980s

After independence in 1973, some Bahamians felt that they did not want to be service providers for visitors from the world's powerful colonising countries. At the same time, oil prices went up, making travel more expensive. Many other Caribbean countries were marketing themselves as holiday destinations, so there was stiff competition in the region. All these changes discouraged tourists.

However, between 1969 and 1979, the government set up a huge project to conduct market research. The results were used to improve tourism in The Bahamas through staff training, courtesy campaigns and new tourist programmes in hotels.

▲ A luxury cruise ship

In the 1980s, huge cruise ships became a more common sight in the Caribbean, bringing thousands of visitors. This was also an era where celebrity musicians came to the Caribbean to record music, to enjoy lavish holidays and to buy property. Many also benefitted from lower tax rates in the Caribbean.

1990s and 2000s

The development of the internet, email and mobile phone technology from the 1990s onwards greatly changed the way people could book and plan travel and accommodation.

Activity 2 A timeline of the history of tourism

1 Why was Sir Stafford Sands known as the 'Father of Tourism'?
2 Draw a timeline of some of the main events in the development of the tourism industry in The Bahamas.

Activity 3 Create a market research form

Imagine that your task is to make suggestions for how The Bahamas can attract more tourists. In order to do this, you decide to conduct market research by interviewing guests at several resorts. You need to find out information about where they are from, why they are travelling, how long they are staying, and what their experiences have been like, in the country and in the resort.

Create a market research form. Your questions should be clear, and you should use a combination of different kinds of questions: yes/no questions, rating scales from 1 to 5, ordering from most to least important, checklists and questions with open fields for answers.

The importance of tourism

The tourism industry brings many benefits. The main benefit is income. Almost half of the money earned in The Bahamas comes from tourism. Visitors spend more than 2 billion dollars each year. The **labour force** is all the people in a country who are able to work, including those who may be unemployed. The **workforce** refers to people who actually have jobs or work and earn money.

Another benefit is improved **infrastructure** – the physical structures and facilities that make it possible for tourists to arrive and stay here. This includes, for example:

- new, improved and rebuilt docks and harbours
- bigger, better airports
- updated transport systems, including roads and bridges
- improved communication systems such as cellular networks
- resorts, hotels and guest houses.

Tourism has also brought improved education and training. For example, the Hotel Training School offers courses that train people for jobs in hotels, restaurants and resorts. The College of The Bahamas also offers degree and certification programmes to train people in hotel management as well as catering.

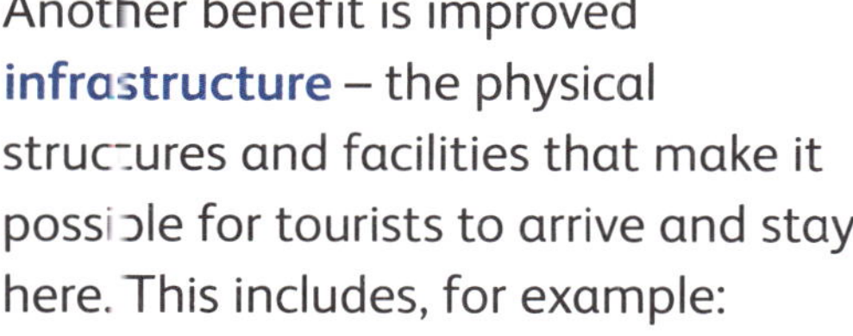

Word power

labour force
workforce
infrastructure

The industries people work in (2011)

▲ Catering is an important aspect of tourism

Activity 4 How tourism helps The Bahamas

1. In 2020, the Covid-19 pandemic stopped millions of tourists from travelling to the Caribbean. Discuss with your family the impact this had on The Bahamas. Write a short essay about this topic.

2. Discuss disadvantages that tourism may bring. Use these ideas to help you:

   impact on wildlife   effects on beaches

   cost of food   traffic   pollution

3. Has tourism brought any changes to your island in the last five years? If so, describe them and explain how they may have changed the lives of people who live there.

Word power
ambassador

Reflection
How would your life in The Bahamas change if we no longer had tourists coming into the country?

Jobs in tourism

The tourist industry is a very important source of work for Bahamians. Many people work in hotels, restaurants, tour services, information and booking services, taxi services, and many other jobs. Everyone who works in the tourist industry is an **ambassador** for our country. Tourists bring employment and prosperity to our country. It is important to welcome them with hospitality, friendliness and excellent service.

Activity 5 Services for tourists

1 Look at these photographs.

   a Write a sentence about the services that you can see in each photograph.

   b List some other services that tourists need or use.

A

B

C

D

2 The pictures below show some people who work in the tourist industry. Match each of the following jobs to the number of the matching picture.

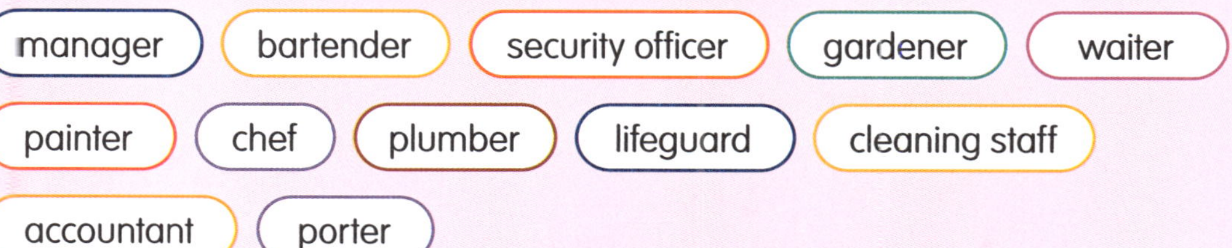

manager　　bartender　　security officer　　gardener　　waiter

painter　　chef　　plumber　　lifeguard　　cleaning staff

accountant　　porter

3 a Imagine that you are a guest at a hotel or resort. Which staff members are you likely to speak to the most?

b Which other jobs have less direct contact with guests, but are still important to keep the hotel running smoothly?

4 Why is it especially important for Bahamians who work in the tourist industry to excel at their work?

5 Draw two flow diagrams to show:

a how excellent service helps to grow our tourist industry and benefit Bahamians

b how poor service does the opposite.

Think about the effect that service has on each guest's experience, how they might respond during and after their trip, the image of The Bahamas abroad, future tourist bookings, and jobs for Bahamians.

In this unit, you will:

- examine the different ways people reach The Bahamas (by air, by ship)
- sequence the process travellers use (passport, baggage, money exchange)
- discuss advances in international transportation and communication.

International transport and communication

Forms of **transportation** are ways to move **passengers** and **cargo** from one place to another. The Bahamas is surrounded by sea on all sides. The only way to reach our country is by sea or by air.

The Bahamas is close to the USA, which has very big international airports that connect to the rest of the world. This makes it easy for people and goods to travel quickly and easily between The Bahamas and other countries around the world.

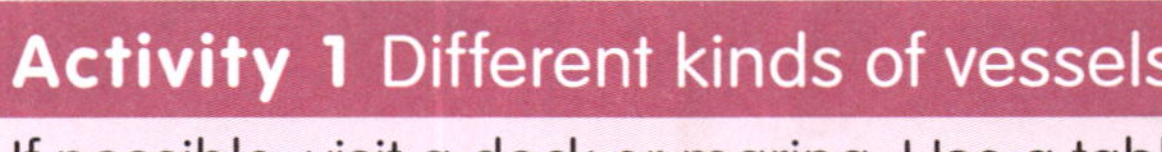

▲ **Sea vessels** include many different kinds of boats and ships. Air transport includes planes of all sizes

Word power

transportation
passenger
cargo
sea vessel

Activity 1 Different kinds of vessels

If possible, visit a dock or marina. Use a table like the one below to help you note the different types of sea vessels you see, how many of each you count, and where they come from.

Type of vessel	Number	Country/flag
Cruise ship		
Freight container		
Fishing trawler		
Sailboat		
Yacht		
Catamaran		
Other		

If your island has an airport, you could visit it. List the countries that the planes come from.

Communication technology

Communication technology allows us to send and receive information. It also makes travel and transport safer and easier than in the past.

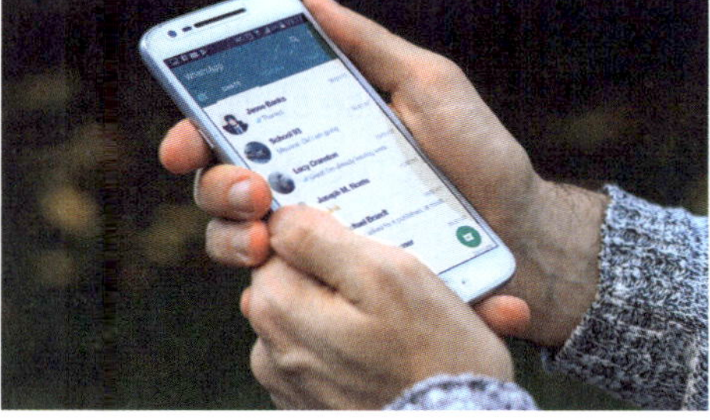

▲ Mobile phone technology

▲ Online banking

▲ Online booking platforms for transport and accommodation

▲ Global Positioning System (GPS)

▲ Radio signals (radar) used by air traffic controllers

▲ Weather warning systems

Activity 2 Using communication technology

1 If possible, use an app on a phone to look up an address in your neighbourhood, such as your home or school. Talk about how a visitor to The Bahamas would be able to use this app, and what makes it easy to use.

2 Look at the pictures above. Explain how each type of technology makes transport or travel safer and/or easier.

3 Look at a weather app or information system. Write a paragraph giving five items of information you found out.

Arriving by ship

A cruise ship is a kind of floating hotel resort. It may carry between 3000 and 6000 passengers. The ship has several levels or decks. Passengers stay in rooms or cabins with beds called berths. The most expensive cabins are on the upper decks where they have a view of the ocean. They are also cooler and lighter than the lower cabins. Cruise ships have many facilities to cater for their guests, including restaurants, lounges, bars, ballrooms, cinemas, swimming pools, casinos and gyms.

Around 70% of visitors to The Bahamas arrive by cruise ship. Most of these visitors come from the USA. The ships dock at many different islands and cays. Passengers leave the ship for a few hours for sightseeing, gambling and evening entertainment at restaurants, bars and nightclubs. They may also do shopping for souvenirs and other goods. They spend less money than visitors who arrive by plane, because they do not use hotels or resorts.

▲ **Cruise ships bring large numbers of tourists to The Bahamas**

Activity 3 Cruise ships

1 Look at the cruise ship in the picture above. List four differences you notice between this boat and a ferry or mailboat.

2 This table shows a summary of cruise visitors to The Bahamas from 2016 to 2021.

Cruise visitors by first port of entry			
Year	Total Bahamas	Nassau/Providence Island	Grand Bahama	Out Islands
2016	4,690, 374	2,557,973	614,620	1,517,781
2017	4,626,259	2,637,243	467,289	1,521,727
2018	4,877,596	2,596,687	514,112	1,766,797
2019	5,433,359	2,877,364	416,287	2,139,708
2020	1,327,142	576,318	91,274	659,550
2021	1,115,181	450,213	45,202	619,766

a In which year did Grand Bahama receive its highest number of visitors?

b In which year did the whole country receive its highest number of visitors?

c Between which two years did the number of visitors to the Out Islands increase the most?

d The Covid-19 pandemic had a serious effect on tourism. Use the numbers from the table to explain what happened to tourism, and why.

e In which year was there more than half a million more visitors to The Bahamas than the previous year?

Arriving by air

Our national airline is Bahamasair. It has planes that fly to many of our islands. Charter companies, such as Southern Air, Pineapple Air, Western Air and Sky Bahamas, also offer flights. Some individuals own private planes.

▲ Bahamasair plane bringing tourists to The Bahamas

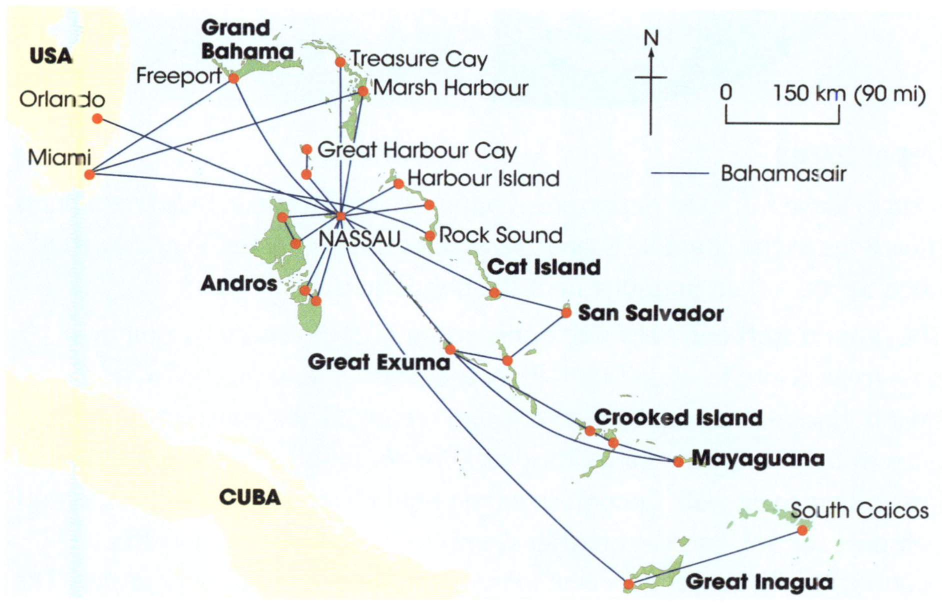

▲ Map of flight routes to the islands

An airport has two main areas – arrivals and departures. Passengers have to follow a series of specific steps when they enter or leave the country at an airport. The information that follows explains the steps that passengers follow when they arrive and when they leave.

Arrivals

When a plane lands, the passengers disembark and enter through arrivals. They may need to hand in a health declaration to a health officer. International visitors must go through passport control, where an immigration officer checks their documents. Most visitors do not need a special visa to visit The Bahamas. They receive a stamp in their passport to show they have entered the country.

Next, the passengers collect their luggage from the baggage carousel. They take it past the customs officer, who checks that no prohibited or dangerous items are brought into the country. Sometimes the officer may stop a passenger and search their bag.

Word power

visa

Connections

This woman works as an immigration officer. Can you think of other people who work as ground staff in the arrivals section?

Once passengers have arrived, they may need to exchange money. Outside the airport or passenger terminal, porters work to help passengers carry their bags to taxis or hotel shuttles.

Departures

Visitors leave from the departures section. The porters can help them bring their bags to the check-in. Even if passengers have checked in online, they need to check their baggage in at the baggage check.

The ground staff can help with questions or booking changes, or if a passenger is late for their flight. After the passenger is checked in and their baggage checked, they go through security. Their carry-on luggage goes through X-ray machines that scan for dangerous or prohibited items. Passengers must walk through scanning equipment. Next, they go through passport control, and get another stamp to show they have left the country. Finally, passengers wait in the departures lounge for boarding. The main lounge has restaurants and shops with duty-free shopping. Premium passengers and VIPs may have access to special lounges.

▲ **A tourist checking in baggage**

Activity 4 Procedures at the airport

1 Use the information to help you draw two flow diagrams:
   a each step of the process at the airport for a visitor arriving
   b each step of the process at the airport for a visitor leaving The Bahamas.
2 Around your flow diagrams, list the different jobs that Bahamians may do at each step.

Activity 5 Role play

1 Role play a family arriving at the airport. First act out a scene where workers at the airport are rude and unhelpful. Then act out another scene where everyone is friendly and helpful. Discuss how each experience would make the family feel.
2 Write down five different jobs of people who work at airports. For each one, explain how they can make tourists feel welcome.

Reflection

How have advances in technology and communication made it easier for people to travel?

11 Farming and fishing

In this unit, you will:

- identify the economic impact of farming and fishing in The Bahamas
- compare past and present methods of farming
- categorise different types of livestock farming, and identify islands where livestock is farmed
- discuss ways we preserve the economic value of farming.

The importance of fishing

Our fishermen rely on three main fishing grounds: the Great Bahama Bank, the Little Bahama Bank and Cay Sal Bank. Spanish Wells, Long Island, Abaco and Andros are the islands where most fishing takes place.

A lot of our fish and seafood gets transported by mail boat from the Family Islands to the main market at New Providence.

The main products we catch and export are crawfish (spiny lobster), fish and conch. We export a lot of fish and seafood, and this brings foreign exchange into the country. Most of our seafood is exported to the USA.

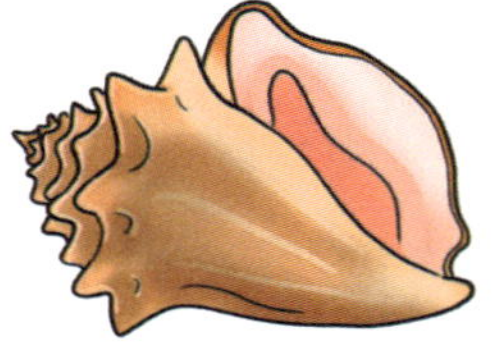

Activity 1 Fishing in The Bahamas

1 Locate the three main banks on a map. Identify which is closest to your island.

2 Look at the graphs below. Then answer the questions that follow.

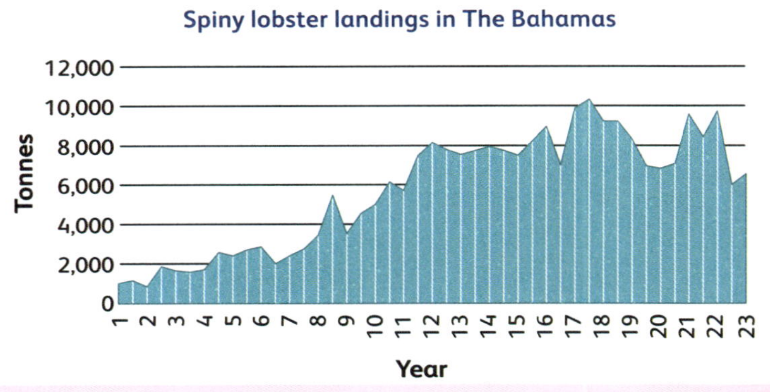

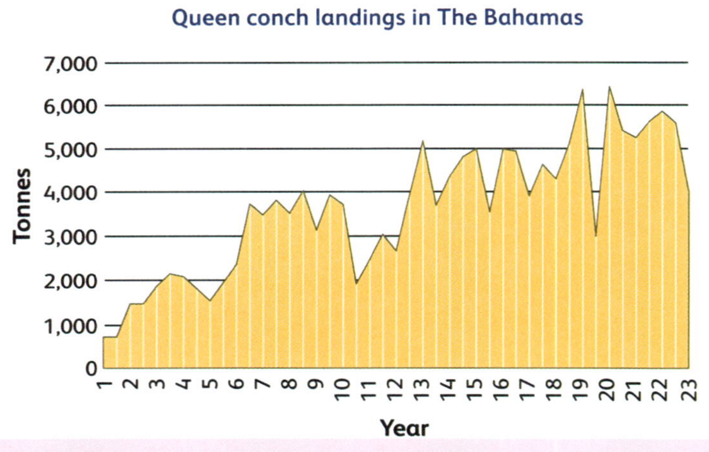

Did you know?

In 2020, the Agriculture and Marine Resources Minister announced that the government was planning to end conch exports. Tourists would no longer be allowed to harvest conch. Use the internet to find out what has been done since then to protect different marine (ocean) resources in our country.

a Explain in your own words what we mean by landings when we talk about fishing.

b Describe the main pattern you notice in the harvesting of seafood from the graphs above.

c If we had data for a further 40 years, do you think it would show that the landings would keep increasing, or start decreasing? Why do you think so?

3 Write your own definitions of the following terms:

a overfishing

b closed season.

Farming in The Bahamas

Crop farming

Crop farming means growing plants for food or for other products. We categorise crops in several different ways

- Fruits and vegetables are grown as food, whereas **field crops**, such as coffee, tobacco, cotton and sugar, are usually used to make other products. Our main field crop in The Bahamas is sugar.
- We grow tree fruits, such as oranges, lemons and coconuts, and vine fruits, such as grapes, melons, dragonfruit and passionfruit.
- **Export crops** are grown to sell to other countries. Our main export crops are grapefruit, limes, okra, papaya, pineapples and avocado. Other crops are grown for **local consumption**. Many of these are traditional crops, such as cassava, sweet potato, cabbage, sweet peppers, goat peppers, pigeon peas, corn, okra and tomatoes.

Livestock farming

Livestock are animals that we farm for their meat or products such as milk, eggs, feathers, wool and leather. We categorise livestock into different sub-groups:

- Poultry are birds such as chickens, as well as hens, turkeys, geese and ducks. We raise them for their eggs and meat. Poultry farms are mostly located in New Providence and Grand Bahama. Each year, Bahamian farmers produce thousands of tonnes of chicken meat, and millions of eggs.
- Many pig farms are in New Providence. Pigs are our second-most important type of livestock.
- Cattle are the cows and calves farmed for milk and beef. Cow milk is the main ingredient in dairy products such as cheese, butter and yoghurt. Beef cattle are farmed in North Andros and New Providence.
- Goats and sheep, also farmed in New Providence, provide meat as well as milk that can also be used for cheeses.

Word power

crop farming
field crop
export crops
local consumption
livestock

Activity 2 A class survey

1 a Do you know anyone who works in the fishing or farming industries? As a class, identify how many of you know someone who works in one of these industries.

b As a class, draw a tally chart or pictograph to represent how many people you know work in each of these industries: tourism, banking, fishing, farming, manufacturing, retail.

2 Look at the labels of some dairy products. Identify the countries we get the following products from: butter, cream, milk and yoghurt.

Activity 3 Farming in The Bahamas

Have a class discussion about farming on your island. Discuss:

1 What kinds of farming took place historically (in the past) on your island?

2 What kind of farming takes place today?

3 About how many people do you think work in agriculture on your island?

4 Which products can you buy that are farmed on your island?

5 What is the difference in price between locally grown and imported produce? Why?

6 If farming does not take place on your island, which is the nearest island that does have farming activity?

You may not know the answers to all these questions. Discuss how you could find out more.

Past and present farming practices

Look at some of the ways farming practices have changed over time.

▲ In the past, farmers had to save seed from each harvest to plant for the following year. Today, companies produce seeds that are treated to keep them fresh and ensure healthy crop yields. The mass-produced seeds have less genetic diversity than a crop of traditionally harvested seeds.

▲ Soil can get depleted if we grow the same crops year after year. In the past, farmers had to rotate their crops, and sometimes leave some fields to recover. They used chicken manure to enrich the soil. Today, commercially produced fertilisers allow farmers to add nutrients into the soil. However, when fertilisers get into dams and seas, they can cause algae to flourish.

▲ Sometimes pests or diseases attack crops. Modern science has allowed us to develop chemical pesticides. However, these sometimes kill other plants and animals, and upset ecosystems.

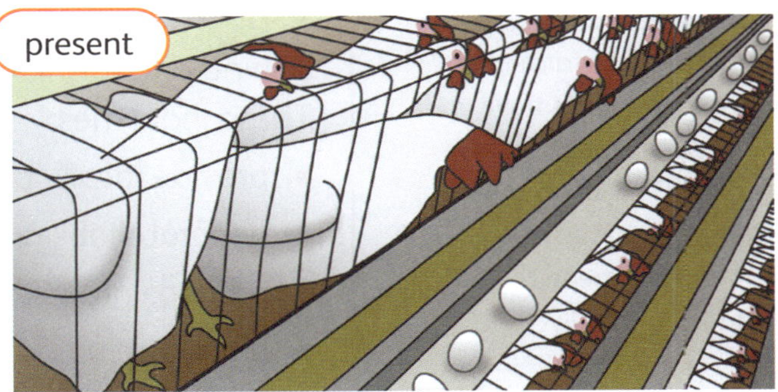

▲ On big, industrial farms, farmers may use intensive farming methods to increase their production. They may pack in more animals in a tighter space. They may inject the livestock with antibiotics to prevent diseases, and hormones to make them grow faster or produce more eggs or milk.

▲ Advances in genetic engineering mean that scientists have developed stronger plants that produce higher yields. This can make the annual production levels more reliable. However, it also reduces biodiversity.

▲ Planting, weeding and harvesting crops can require a lot of manual labour. Modern technology can do some tasks quickly and efficiently using machinery. One example is mechanised harvesting equipment, which harvests sugarcane.

Activity 4 Modern farming practices

1 Explain what you understand by the following terms:

 a local consumption   **b** intensive farming

 c economically viable   **d** sustainable use of resources.

2 Modern agricultural techniques bring many advantages, but they can also introduce problems. Work in pairs or groups. Identify three examples of problems that modern farming practices can cause. Suggest how you would address each problem if you were a farmer.

Reflection

What locally farmed or fished products have you eaten this week or this month? What do our fishing and farming industries mean to you and your family?

Word power

economically viable
migrant workers

Government assistance and control

Fishing and farming are both very important for The Bahamas. These industries:

- provide locally produced, affordable food within our country
- generate jobs and income for many families
- produce products we can trade with other countries
- bring foreign exchange into our country
- provide raw materials for other industries
- motivate our government to encourage sustainable use of resources.

Activity 5 Keeping fishing and farming viable

The Bahamian government understands that it is important to sustain our fishing and farming industries and keep them **economically viable**. In order to do this, each Ministry has a role to play. Work in groups. Each group chooses one of the following questions to research, then reports back to the class.

1 The Ministry of Agriculture and Marine Resources has many rules and restrictions around fishing. These include fishing permits, rules about the types of fishing equipment that may be used to catch fish, and limits on which types of seafood may be caught. Do some research and write a report on the main rules and regulations, and how they aim to keep our fishing resources sustainable.

2 What does the Ministry of Agriculture do to help farmers modernise their farming practices? Conduct research online to find out, or ask someone who works in the farming industry to speak to your class.

3 People who travel to a country to work there temporarily are known as **migrant workers**. The Ministry of Immigration limits the number of migrant farm workers in The Bahamas. Find out the main rules for migrant workers coming to The Bahamas. Explain why you think the government does this.

4 The Bahamas Ministry of Agriculture and Marine Resources has a YouTube channel where they upload videos. Watch one of the videos on this channel. Write a paragraph summarising what the video told you about government support for farming and fishing in The Bahamas.

12 Government and citizens

In this unit, you will:
- identify our government leaders and discuss their roles
- discuss the rights and responsibilities of citizens
- distinguish between laws and rules
- explain the consequences of breaking rules and laws
- analyse causes of conflict and ways of resolving conflicts
- discuss global events.

Our leaders

At election time, Bahamian people vote to elect the head of our government, the Prime Minister. He or she also takes the role of Minister of Finance, as well as Member of Parliament for New Providence and Abaco.

Because we are a Commonwealth country, our official Chief of State is the monarch (king or queen) of Britain. Until 2022, this was Queen Elizabeth II, and after her death, King Charles III. The Governor-General represents King Charles in The Bahamas. This is mostly a symbolic and ceremonial role. The Prime Minister must formally recommend the Governor-General to the monarch, before the Governor-General is appointed. Sometimes a Governor-General has had a career as an MP, but this is not always the case.

This list shows our first twelve Governors-General since independence:

▲ A statue honouring Sir Milo Butler, who served as Minister of Health and Welfare, Minister of Labour, and Minister of Agriculture and Fisheries before he eventually became Governor-General

Name	Date
Sir John Warburton Paul (acting Governor-General)	10 – 31 July 1973
Sir Milo Boughton Butler First	1 August 1973 – 22 January 1979
Sir Gerald Cash	22 January 1979 – 25 June 1988
Sir Henry Milton Taylor	26 June 1988 – 1 January 1992
Sir Clifford Darling	2 January 1992 – 2 January 1995
Sir Orville Turnquest	3 January 1995 – 13 November 2001
Dame Ivy Dumont	13 November 2001 – 30 November 2005
The Hon. Paul L. Adderley (acting Governor-General)	1 December 2005 – 1 February 2006
The Hon. Arthur Dion Hanna	1 February 2006 – 14 April 2010
Sir Arthur Foulkes	14 April 2010 – 7 July 2014
Dame Marguerite Pindling	8 July 2014 – 28 June 2019
Sir Cornelius A. Smith	28 June 2019 –

Activity 1 Know your leaders

1 Use the list on the previous page to answer these questions:

   a Who kept the title of Governor-General for the longest period?

   b What is the more usual period that a Governor-General stays in office?

   c The last person in this list is missing the end date of their period as Governor-General. Find out when he ended his term, and who took over after that.

2 Make up a mnemonic to help you recall the names of the Governors-General in order.

3 In class, discuss what the role of the Governor-General is. Talk about what they might do in a day. Dramatise a documentary called 'A day in the life of our Governor-General.'

4 Imagine that your class could take over as Governor-General for one week. Brainstorm what you would try to achieve in that week.

The first five Prime Ministers after independence were:

Rt. Hon. Sir Lyden Oscar Pindling

1972 – 1977;
1977 – 1982;
1982 – 1987;
1987 – 1992
(5 terms)

Rt. Hon Hubert Alexander Ingraham

1992 – 2002;
2007 – 2012
(2 terms)

Rt. Hon. Perry Gladstone Christie

2002 – 2007;
2012 – 2017
(2 terms)

Most Rt. Hon. Hubert Alexander Minnis

2017 – 2021
(1 term)

Rt. Hon. Philip Edward Davis

2021 – 2025
(current term at time of writing)

Activity 2 The role of the Prime Minister

1 The Prime Minister's job is different to that of the Governor-General. Use the information on the previous page. In groups, play a guessing game. Take turns to make statements based on the information you have about the different roles. The rest of the group must guess whether you are the PM or the GG.

2 What does the Minister of Youth, Sports and Culture do? Look in a newspaper, and try to find current news that mentions this minister. Share with the class what you found.

3 Pretend you are making an advertisement for the position of Prime Minister *OR* Dramatise a short 'day in the life of the PM' skit to show candidates what they should be able to do.

4 Write a letter to the Prime Minister with an outline for an important project you would like them to consider.

Understanding our rights

Human rights are those things which all people should be able to have and enjoy, which no one can take away. For example, all people have the right to live freely without fear of unfair or violent treatment. Some rights should be enjoyed by all people on Earth. These rights are set out in The Universal Declaration of Human Rights, drawn up by the United Nations.

> **Word power**
>
> human rights

The Universal Declaration of Children's Rights

All children have the right to a name, enough to eat and a place to live.

All children should be looked after when they are sick, and have a right to grow up with love, affection and security.

Disabled children have a right to special treatment and education.

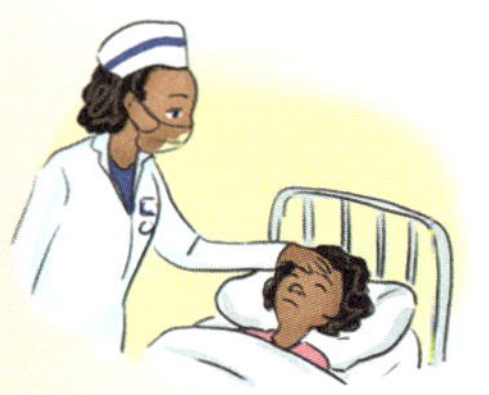

All children have a right to free education and should be protected from neglect, cruelty and exploitation.

All children should not be made to work before a certain age and should be protected from discrimination.

All children should never have to fear arrest and detention, and should be brought up to understand that their energy and their talents should be devoted to the service of their brothers and sisters.

Activity 3 Children's rights

1 Read the summary of the rights in the Universal Declaration of Children's Rights above. Discuss with your group why you think each of these rights are especially important for children.

2 True or false? Explain your answer for each statement.

- From the age of 11 upwards, all children should be allowed to vote.
- All children need a safe, loving home.
- Children must work as soon as they are ready.
- No one must harm children.
- You shouldn't help anyone except your own family.

Balancing rights and responsibilities

Many individual countries, including The Bahamas, have their own **Constitution**. This is a document that sets out the rights of its **citizens**. Bahamians all have the right to:

▲ freedom of speech

▲ freedom of religion

▲ freedom of political preference

▲ protection of property and privacy

Together with rights, we have **responsibilities**. A responsibility is a duty. It is something you need to do or take care of. Here are some examples of rights balanced by responsibilities.

The right to ...	Responsibility
Freedom	Respect other people's rights and freedom, follow the law, and do not harm others
Free speech and personal expression	Respect others and refrain from hate speech
Practise your chosen religion	Respect the religions of others and allow them to practise their own religion freely
Privacy	Respect the privacy of others

Activity 4 Know your rights and responsibilities

Work in pairs.

1 Discuss what happens when a citizen does not uphold their responsibilities. What are the consequences for the individual, and for the community?

2 Design a poster that clearly sets out the rights of a citizen of The Bahamas. On your poster, illustrate the main rights listed in our Constitution. Add your ideas about the responsibilities we have to balance with each right.

When people break the law

Think about the different places in your life where there are rules you need to follow. We follow rules at school and at home, and even when we play games with our friends. Similarly, a government creates a set of rules called **laws**. These are the rules to keep the society functioning well. If you break the law, you may face **consequences**, depending on the circumstances and seriousness of the situation.

The police may arrest lawbreakers and take them to a holding cell at a prison. The **accused** must appear before a magistrate and make a **plea** of **guilty** (no contest) or not guilty. If they plead guilty or no contest to the charges, there is no trial, and they receive a **sentence**. If they plead not guilty, they may have to wait for a trial. The outcome of the trial will determine the sentence.

There are three correctional institutions in The Bahamas:

- the state prison, Bahamas Department of Correctional Services, for adults
- Simpson Penn Centre for boys
- Willie Mae Pratt Centre for girls.

All three are located in the Fox Hill area of New Providence.

> **Word power**
>
> law
> consequence
> accused
> plea
> guilty
> sentence

Activity 5 Laws and correctional institutions

1. Trace the island of New Providence from your atlas. Mark the locations of the three correctional institutions, and label them correctly.

2. Prepare questions you would like to ask a police officer about their job. If possible, invite a police officer to visit your class and answer the questions.

3. Write a one-page description of a day in the life of a police officer, or draw a cartoon strip illustrating what they might do in a day.

◀ Bahamas Central Police Station

Conflict resolution

A **conflict** is a disagreement, or a clash of differing views. We all have conflicts sometimes. Conflicts usually arise from differences of opinion, misunderstandings, or disagreements over land and other resources. Some groups have conflict over differing religious or political views. Conflicts may take place among family members, friends or members of a community. Some conflicts arise between different countries.

Activity 6 Causes of conflict

1 In groups, discuss each picture. Identify the main cause of the conflict, and how it could be resolved.

▲ Conflict between siblings

▲ Conflict between neighbours

▲ Conflict between different interest groups, such as businesses and environmental activists

▲ Conflicts between people and governments

Different ways to handle conflict

Different people handle disagreements in different ways. Some ways of handling conflict cause greater conflict and more problems. Others help to resolve the conflict.

- To escalate conflict means to make it bigger. Getting angry with someone, shouting, or reacting in an aggressive way are all examples of escalating conflict. Usually, escalation is unhelpful.
- To de-escalate a conflict means to reduce the force of the conflict.
- Resolving a conflict means finding a way to overcome the conflict, usually by finding a solution that both parties can accept.
- Mediators are people who help parties to overcome their conflict through dialogue and mutual understanding.
- If both parties feel heard and understood, they may be able to reach an understanding. This may involve compromise.

▲ Share or take turns

▲ Find other people to spend time with

Activity 7 Resolving conflict

Look at the pictures of ways people try to resolve conflicts. For each picture, suggest the kind of situation where this might help.

▲ Discussion

▲ Think it over or write out your thoughts

▲ Take a deep breath and count to 10

▲ Talk to an adult or authority figure

Activity 8 Community conflict

1 Discuss a conflict that might happen in a community. Come up with your own ideas, or use one of these ideas as a starting point:

- pets are going into neighbours' gardens and digging up plants
- vegetables are going missing from a household garden
- an elderly neighbour complains about the noise caused by young children next door
- homeowners object to a proposed hotel because it will cause an increase in traffic in their area.

Dramatise or role play the conflict. Then brainstorm ways that the people involved might resolve the problem.

2 When do you think conflict might lead to a change in the law? Imagine that you were a community leader. What new law might you suggest to help resolve conflict in the community?

Conflict and global events

The most serious conflicts happen on a larger scale: between communities or between countries. You may learn more about **global events** from news sources on television, on the internet, or in newspapers. This map shows some of the places that were facing serious conflicts in 2022.

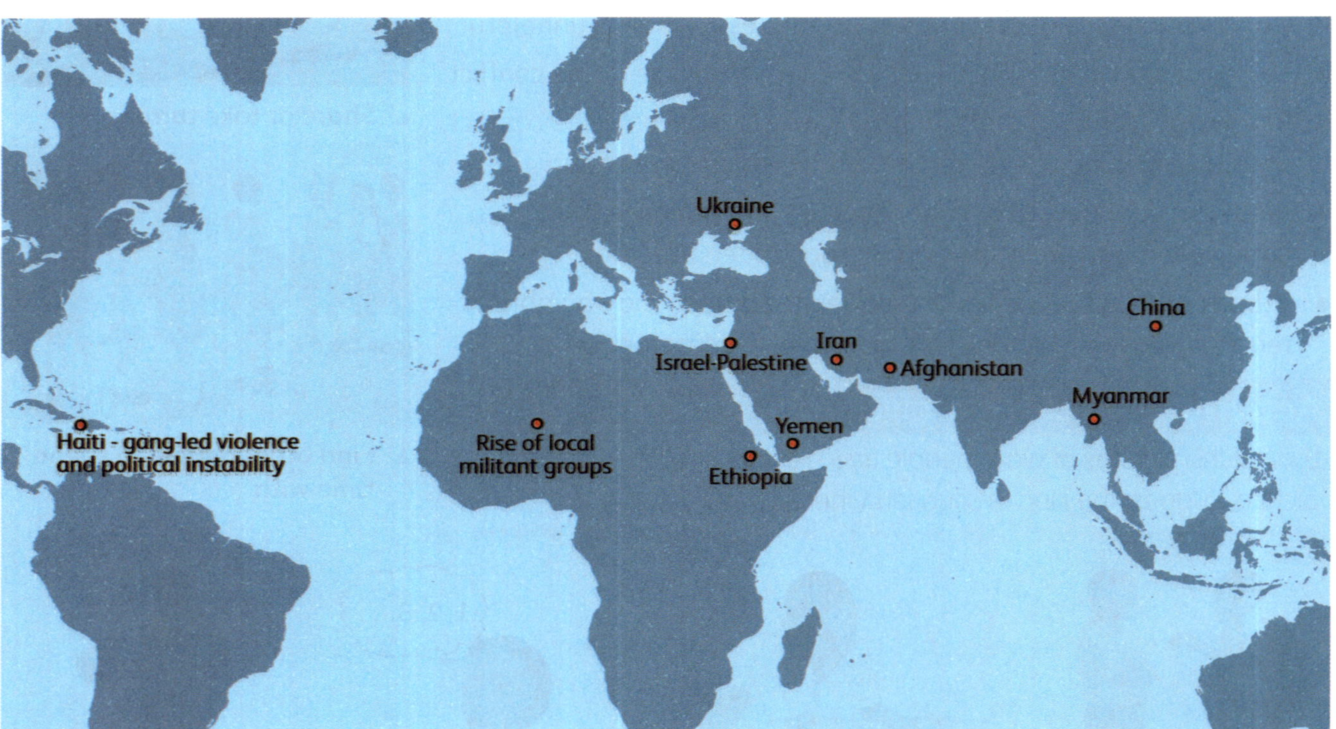

Activity 9 Current issues

1 As a class, watch some news bulletins from a trusted international news source, such as CNN, the BBC or Al-Jazeera.

   a Which countries are in the news this month, and why?

   b Name three other places around the world that are currently in situations of war or conflict.

   c What are the main issues or causes of conflict in each place?

   d As a class, discuss how you would order these stories from most to least important. Explain how you decided.

2 Choose one of the countries listed on the map above. Find out more about the situation in that country. Write a summary of the main conflicts facing the country, and what the situation is currently is.

3 As a class, create an 'Issue of the month' display, with information about an issue currently getting a lot of attention in the international news.

Theme 2 What have you learnt?

Unit 7 Geography of The Bahamas

1 Name:
   a the ocean bank that surrounds the west side of Andros
   b the ocean bank that is towards the north of The Bahamas
   c the long deep area of ocean to the east of Andros.
2 In your own words, explain the difference between weather and climate.

Unit 8 Natural resources and food production

3 List three important natural resources we have in The Bahamas. For each resource, list three jobs it provides.
4 Explain what harvesting means. Give three examples of ways we harvest natural resources.
5 Name three foods that we usually buy in bottles or cans.

Unit 9 Tourism

6 Explain in your own words each of these types of tourists:
   a domestic tourist   b business tourist
   c eco-tourist   d cultural tourist.
7 Most of our tourists come from one country. Name the country and explain why it is the source of most of our tourists.
8 Identify three reasons Sir Stafford Sands was known as 'the father of tourism' in The Bahamas.
9 Draw a mind map or diagram showing at least five benefits that tourism brings to our country.

Unit 10 Transport and communication

10 Which forms of international transportation are used to reach The Bahamas?
11 Write a paragraph discussing three advances in either transportation or communication since the 1950s.

Unit 11 Farming and fishing

12 Fishing is very important to The Bahamas. Explain three ways it benefits our country.
13 Give two examples of each type of crop:
   a traditional crops   b export crops   c field crops.
14 Which is our most important type of livestock farming?
15 Outline three ways that the government helps to preserve the economic value of fishing and farming.

Unit 12 Government and citizenship

16 What is the difference between a Governor-General and a Prime Minister?
17 List three rights that are protected by the Constitution of The Bahamas.

13 Family names

In this unit, you will:
- review Bahamian names and their origins
- link surnames to their origins in our history.

Tracing the heritage of our names

Have you ever guessed which island someone comes from based on their surname?

Case study

The Old Inhabitants of Long Island

The Bahamas were not empty islands when the Loyalists arrived. The people living here included descendants of early European settlers. The Loyalists looked down on these white Bahamians, who were known as Conchs.

Although most of the Eleutherans left The Bahamas before the Loyalists arrived, there were some that stayed. Others who left also returned later, so some names from these settlers may also sound familiar to you. Some families moved to Bermuda and kept close ties to The Bahamas, and then moved back later.

The Long Island Bahamas History project has done research, focusing on Old Inhabitants of Long Island in particular. This map of the island shows how the land was divided into plots and given out to grantees (people or families who received land grants). You can find more information on the Long Island Bahamas History website.

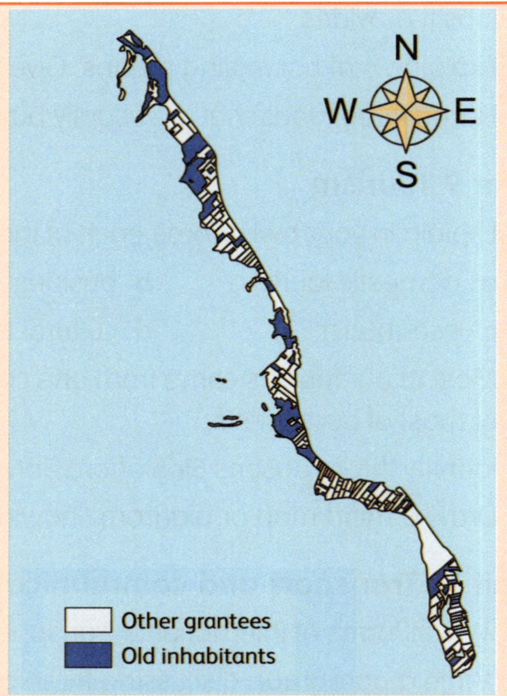

▲ A map of Long Island in the 1780s, showing the main plot divisions between Old Inhabitants and other grantees

Some names of Old Inhabitant families on Long Island

Adderley	Bow/Bowe	Bowles	Brown	Bullard	Bunch
Culmer	Curtis	Darville/Darvil/Darvill		Fox	
Griffin/Griffith		Hewitt/Hewet	Hunt		
Johnson/Johnston/Johnstone		Knowles	Maycock	McKenzie	
McKinney/McKenney/McKeney		Newton	Pritchard	Smith	
Thompson	Wells	Wilson	Young		

Names of Eleutheran Adventurers

Bethell	Carey	Charlow	Culmer	Dorsett
Ingraham	Kemp	Knowles	Lowe	Newbold Pinder
Sands	Sawyer	Watkins		

Thousands of Loyalists and enslaved people settled on different islands. Some of the more famous Loyalists were John Russell in Abaco, Dennis Rolle in Exuma, Robert Curry in New Providence, Alexander Collie in Crooked Island, and Wyannie Malone in Hope Town. It was common for enslaved people to take the surnames of their owners.

Joseph Curry moved from Glasgow, Scotland, to America around 1750. He lived in South Carolina. He and his wife, Jane Curry, had six sons: Joseph, John, Richard, Benjamin, William and Stephan. After the war, five of the sons moved to The Bahamas, while Jane and Stephan stayed in America. William Curry became a merchant in Nassau. The other four brothers lived on Harbour Island. Later Richard and Benjamin both married Conchs and moved to Green Turtle Cay, Abaco. Benjamin had two children: Jane Curry, and Benjamin Curry, who in turn also married a Conch, Martha Albury, and had a son, William Curry. William moved to Key West in Florida and became a well-known merchant, shipbuilder, wrecker and public official. People called him "Rich Bill" or "Florida's first millionaire".

Activity 1

1 Read the extract above. What does it tell you about the origins of people with the surname Curry?

2 Interview some of your older family members. Find out as much as you can about the names (surnames and first names) of people in your family.

3 Research the origins of your family name. Perhaps you have one of the names you have seen in this unit, or perhaps your family has its own different story. You can do research by speaking to family members, looking online, or look at history books in your local library.

4 Draw up a family tree. Add flags of the islands where your family members lived.

Connections

Reflection

If you could go back in time and speak to your ancestors, what would you choose to ask them?

14 Nation builders

What is a nation builder?

We use the term **nation builder** for people who work hard to achieve very highly in their field, and who bring excellence and success to our country. Every person, young and old, who lives in The Bahamas has their own special contribution to make towards building and growing our nation. We can all be nation builders.

Word power

nation builder

Activity 1 Research the life and contribution of a nation builder

Choose one of the nation builders on these pages, or another of your own choice. In groups, research that person's life and achievements. Present your work in a poster or booklet, or as a digital presentation. You should include:

- the field of contribution to nation building (for example: sports, music, art, religion, education or social activism)
- the background and life story of the person
- important events in their life
- how they have had an impact on Bahamian society and culture today.

In sports

▲ Ariana Vanderpool-Wallace, swimming champion

► Antoan Richardson, baseball player and coach (b. 1983)

▲ Deandre Ayton, basketball player (b. 1998)

▲ Jazz Chisholm, baseball player (b. 1998)

▲ Jonquel Jones, basketball player (b. 1994)

▲ Tureano Johnson, boxer (b. 1984)

In music

▲ Blake Alphonso Higgs, also known as "Blind Blake" (1915–1986)

▲ Angelique Sabrina, singer, songwriter, dancer, actress and performer (b. 1998)

▲ Joseph Spence, guitarist and singer (1910–1984)

In art

▲ Anina Major, sculptor and visual artist (b. 1981)

▲ Tamika Galanis, documentarian and multimedia visual artist

▲ Stanley Burnside, painter, art teacher and cartoonist (b. 1947)

In literature and film

▶ Marion Bethel, attorney, human rights activist, writer and filmmaker (b. 1953)

▶ Sidney Poitier, actor, director and diplomat (1927–2022)

Social and religious leaders

▲ Bishop Michael Hartley Eldon – first Anglican Bishop to serve in Bahamas

▲ Sir Etienne Dupuch, newspaper editor and anti-discrimination activist who later became a Member of Parliament (1899–1991)

▲ William Edwards Thompson, priest and community leader (1933–2000)

Activists for social change

▲ Er n Greene, human rights advocate

▲ Allyson Maynard Gibson, barrister, politician and human rights activist (b. 1957)

▲ Dellon Evans, climate activist and youth ambassador (b. 2007)

Activity 2 Explore your own ideas for nation building

In groups, discuss these questions:

1 'You are never too young or too old to make a difference.' How do the examples on these pages support this statement?

2 If you could make a positive change to your community, which of these areas would you choose to focus on? As a group, decide which area or topic is most important to you.

- environmental awareness
- fighting climate change
- road safety
- gender equality
- voter education
- Bahamian culture and heritage
- human rights
- child safety

3 Discuss in your group what you could do to make a difference in the area you chose. Plan a project or activity that will help you to become the nation builder you would like to be.

Reflection

Has this unit made you think differently about what it means to be a nation builder? How could you help to be a nation builder?

15 Junkanoo

Origins of Junkanoo

▲ **Junkanoo costumes are colourful and creative**

Each year, enslaved people were allowed only three days of rest. On two of these days – 26 December and 1 January – they would celebrate with traditional West African masks and costumes, drums and musical instruments. Through music, dance and storytelling, they recounted the story of John Canoe, a famous West African merchant and warrior who fought against Dutch and English colonisers of Ghana. The John Canoe festival was a way for the slaves to express resistance against their oppression. The earliest records of this festival date back to 1769 elsewhere in the Caribbean, and 1801 in The Bahamas. Later it became known as Junkanoo.

The drums and the cowbells create a powerful beat that calls everyone to begin the celebration. We call this a rush-out because people rush into the streets in their multicoloured costumes, and the music and dancing explodes into an unstoppable party. Today, we have Junkanoo marches and celebrations at many different times. We also have school and class rush-outs.

Activity 1 Research Junkanoo origins

Use books or the internet to help you find out more.

1 John Canoe was known by many different names. Find out:

  a some of the different names he was known by

  b more information about John Canoe and why he was considered a hero by the slaves.

2 Research a traditional festival celebrated in Nigeria, Ghana, Benin, Togo or Côte d'Ivoire (Ivory Coast). If possible draw or print a picture of the costumes and masks and describe any similarities you notice to Junkanoo.

Junkanoo instruments

There are different types of musical instruments. Musicians beat or tap percussion instruments to create a rhythm, but these instruments usually have a limited range of notes. Wind instruments are instruments we blow air through, such as horns, flutes and trumpets. In the original Junkanoo festivals, the enslaved people made musical instruments from conch shells, animal horns and poinciana pods. Today, you can hear the 'kalik, kalik' sound of cowbells, and music from a brass band.

▲ Goatskin-covered goombay drum

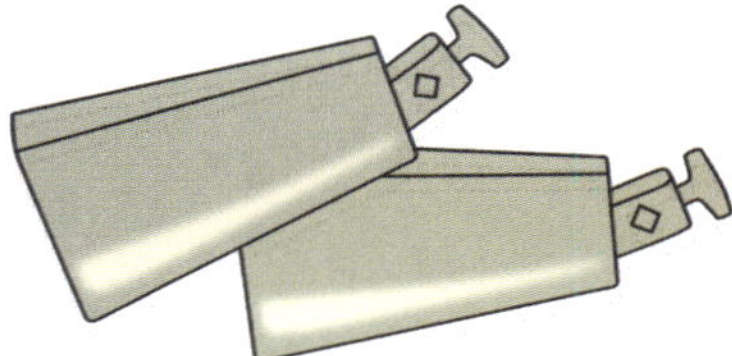

▲ Cowbells

▲ Whistles

▲ The artist Brent Malone made this painting of Junkanoo. Which instruments can you see in the painting?

▲ Trombones, trumpets, tubas and other brass instruments

Activity 2 Junkanoo instruments

1 Discuss with your class the instruments you usually see at Junkanoo. Which of these are:

   a percussion instruments **b** wind instruments?

2 As a class, choose an instrument that you will make for Junkanoo. Decide how you will make it. Collect the materials and create your instrument.

How we paste Junkanoo costumes

In the early days of Junkanoo, enslaved people used any materials they could find to make their costumes. They used powder or flour to paint their faces, and made masks from paper bags or sacks. They also used paper, banana leaves, straw and stones. When sponging was still common, many costumes were made from sponge.

Today, the most common materials are paper, card, glue, wire and crêpe paper. We also add beads, glitter and feathers. Junkanoo costumes must be fringed.

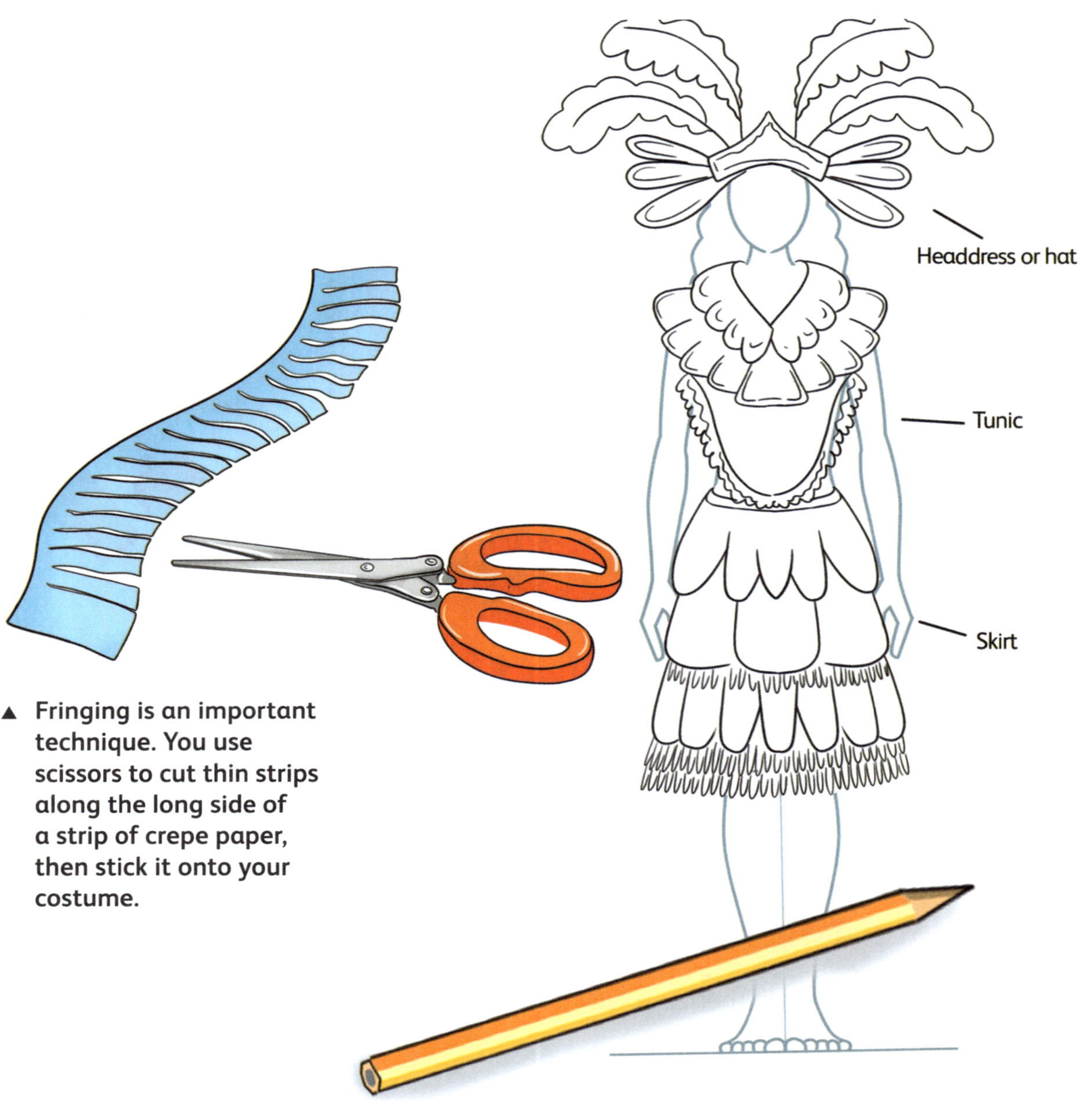

▲ Fringing is an important technique. You use scissors to cut thin strips along the long side of a strip of crepe paper, then stick it onto your costume.

▲ A Junkanoo costume can have many elements. The simplest is just a skirt. But most costumes have a tunic and a headdress too.

▲ Children in bright Junkanoo costumes

Some Junkanoo groups start to design their costumes a year in advance. First, they choose a theme. This will help them to decide on the colour scheme and any special shapes or images. Some themes are simply a colour scheme, such as black and silver. Others use ideas such as fire and water, tropical birds, pirates or African warriors. The possibilities are endless, and the results are always spectacular and colourful.

Activity 3 Junkanoo costumes

1 Imagine you have a cousin living on another island who will be visiting The Bahamas during Junkanoo time. They want to prepare a Junkanoo costume. Write a list of materials they will need. Then write simple instructions, with sketches, to show the method they should use.

2 In groups, plan and create your own costumes for the next Junkanoo.

   a Decide on a theme.

   b Choose colours and images that suit your theme.

   c Design your costumes.

   d Use paper, card, wire, glue and crepe paper to make your costumes.

Reflection

Why is Junkanoo so important to Bahamians? What does it mean to you?

In this unit, you will:
- list public holidays of The Bahamas
- describe Whit Monday activities
- outline the significance of Randol Fawkes Labour Day
- describe festivals and regattas and their significance.

Public holidays

▶ Public holidays are days that remember and honour important days in our history

Public holidays are non-working days. Each country has its own particular set of public holidays. Like many other Christian countries, we have public holidays for the most important days in the Christian calendar such as Good Friday, Whit Monday and Christmas Day.

Other holidays allow us to remember and honour important parts of our history:

- **Majority Rule Day** celebrates the first time that everyone in The Bahamas was allowed to vote, in 1967. It is a way to celebrate fairness, equality and human rights.

- On 10 July 1973, The Bahamas became independent from Britain. We celebrate the same date every year, now known as **Independence Day**, with carnivals, Junkanoo parades and fireworks.

- **Emancipation Day** celebrates the freeing of enslaved people in 1834. We usually mark this event with Junkanoo, going to the beach, and attending regattas.

- **National Heroes' Day** celebrates nation builders and other heroes. There is usually a week-long programme of activities, speeches, family gatherings and picnics around this time.

Activity 1 Categorise public holidays

1 Draw a table with three columns, headed Religious, Political and Historical. Work with a partner. Sort the public holidays in this list into your table. Discuss with your partner why that holiday is important and what we celebrate or commemorate on each day.

Public holidays of The Bahamas

New Year's Day – 1 January

Majority Rule Day – 10 January

Good Friday – the Friday before Easter Sunday (date varies)

Whit Monday – 50 days after Easter Sunday

Randol Fawkes Labour Day – first Friday in June

Independence Day – 10 July

Emancipation Day – First Monday in August

National Heroes' Day – Second Monday in October

Christmas Day – 25 December

Boxing Day – 26 December

2 What does your family do on:

a Whit Monday

b Emancipation Day?

Write a list of the main things that usually happen on that day.

3 Around which public holiday do we hold rush-outs? Write a poem or a song about your own experience of rush-out.

Randol Fawkes Labour Day

Sir Randol Fawkes was an important nation builder in our history. He was a lawyer, and fought for the rights of trade unions and workers. Some people called him 'The Father of Labour'. In 1967, he established a public holiday in honour of workers and unions. This public holiday is now named after him and known as Randol Fawkes Labour Day. Members of the labour unions, political leaders and bands usually parade through Nassau, and leaders give speeches. Many families go to the beach on this day.

▲ Sir Randol Fawkes

▲ A march through downtown Nassau for Randol Fawkes Labour Day

Activity 2 Research Randol Fawkes Labour Day

Choose one of the following ways to do your own research about Randol Fawkes and the labour movement:

Watch YouTube videos of Labour Day marches from previous years. Discuss which parts of the celebrations look similar to other celebrations you have been to.

OR

Research more about the life of Randol Fawkes. You can use books from the library, or websites. Write a fact file about his life.

OR

If possible, your teacher can invite a union representative or labour activist to speak to your class and share more with you about labour issues that affect workers today. Write a summary of what you learnt from their visit.

Festivals

A festival is a cultural celebration, a kind of party for the whole community. You have already learnt about Junkanoo, our most famous festival. Here are some other festivals held each year.

▲ Andros Crab Fest, celebrated at the start of June, with many crab dishes, a display about the life cycle of crabs and the crab-catching industry, and Rake 'n' Scrape performances

▲ Fox Hill Day Festival, celebrated in August. This is the oldest festival in The Bahamas, commemorating the emancipation of enslaved Africans. There are usually prayer services, traditional food and drinks, music and dancing

▲ Bahamas International Film Festival (BIFF), held in December, to showcase films from all over the world

▲ Eleuthera Pineapple Festival, held in the first week of June in Gregory Town, North Eleuthera. You can enjoy pineapples prepared in many different ways, take part in pineapple eating and cooking contests, and in games and sports

▲ E. Clement Bethel National Arts Festival, an annual competition for music, dance, art and drama

▲ Bahamas Coconut Festival, held around Easter time, with many activities and dishes that use coconuts

▲ Conch Festival, held in October. There are competitions for the largest conch, best conch dish and best conch salad, and other activities

▲ Festival of Lights Boat Parade, held in December

Activity 3 Why we hold festivals

1 In groups, discuss which festivals you have attended. What do you remember about them?

2 Why do you think we have festivals? Brainstorm some of the purposes they serve.

3 Choose which Bahamian festival you would most like to attend. Write a paragraph explaining why you find this festival interesting or important.

Regattas

Sailing is important to Bahamians. We sail boats to catch fish and other seafood, and to travel between islands. However, in the 20th century, many boats were in poor condition, or no longer suitable for use. The tradition of boat-building was disappearing.

In 1954, a group of yachtsmen organised a regatta. They aimed to create an event that would bring Bahamians together to enjoy the sport of sailing, and to promote the work of Bahamian boat-builders. It would also create a reason to upgrade the fleet of working sailboats. This event was very successful. Regattas became an annual tradition throughout The Bahamas.

Below are some different types of boats we have in The Bahamas.

▲ Sloop

▲ Schooner

▲ Dinghy

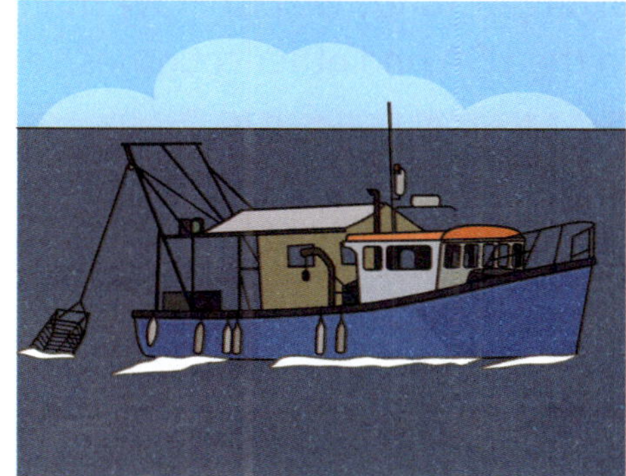

▲ Oyster dredger

> **Reflection**
>
> Why do you think public holidays and festivals differ from one country to another?

Activity 4 Make a model boat

1. Choose one of the types of boats that is familiar to you from around your island. If possible, take photographs that you can use to design a model.

2. Choose your materials. Ice cream sticks, skewer sticks and toothpicks can be useful for masts. You can use cardboard for the hull and twine or wire for rigging. For the inflated part of a dinghy, you could even use a long, thin balloon. You may also need permanent markers, paint, glue and tape.

3. Create your model and display it in your class.

Our local dishes

▲ Conch is a national symbol of The Bahamas, and we make many famous dishes using this ingredient

Each country has its own **cuisine**. This is the way people eat and cook. Local cuisine comes from the ingredients that are available where people live. We are surrounded by the sea, so many typical Bahamian foods use seafood, especially conch.

Our history, tradition and culture also shape our cuisine. Spicy stews and soups, like chicken souse and okra soup, were part of West African culture. Grits and macaroni cheese came from the American south.

We also enjoy many dishes that are made from the fruits that grow in our tropical environment, for example pineapple tarts, banana breads and coconut cakes and cookies. People's taste in food also changes over time, and different cultures influence and change each other. For example, today we also have many kinds of fast food that are popular in the USA and other countries.

Word power

cuisine

Activity 1 My favourite Bahamian foods

1 Do a survey in your class. Ask each student which of the following five dishes is their favourite Bahamian dish. You can collect your data in a tally table like this:

Dish	Tallies	Total
Peas and rice		
Conch salad		
Fish stew		
Fire engine (corned beef and grits or rice)		
Conch chowder		

2 Use the results from your survey to draw a bar graph.

3 Interview an older person or grandparent. Find out what they ate when they were your age. What were their regular foods, and which foods did they eat on special occasions? What was similar and what was different to today?

Activity 2 Music about food

1 On YouTube, you can find the song 'The Buffet' by Eddie Minnis. Listen to this song.

   a What makes it easy to identify the song as Bahamian?

   b Which different nationalities and cuisines does the singer mention?

   c Which typical foods did you recognise from The Bahamas?

▲ Red Conch chowder

▲ Conch salad

▶ Fish and chips

Connections

Activity 3 Exchanging recipes

1 At home, find a recipe that your family usually makes for a typical Bahamian dish. You can use a handwritten family recipe, or a recipe from a book or website. Bring the recipe to school. Compare it with your classmates. What differences do you notice?

2 If possible, your teacher will invite a local chef, cook or food vendor to your class to tell you about local ingredients and recipes. Find out:

   a What are common local ingredients on your island?

   b How are these similar or different to those on other islands in The Bahamas?

3 Choose a recipe to prepare for your class. Have a food tasting day where you work in groups to prepare a range of traditional Bahamian recipes for one another.

Reflection

Imagine you were travelling or in a different country. Which Bahamian foods would you miss the most?

18 Plants of The Bahamas

Word power

flora

The **flora** of a place is the plants that grow there. In The Bahamas, we use the term 'bush' to mean the shrubs and plants that grow in our environment. Because of our tropical climate, plants that grow here need to be able to survive the heat of summer, as well as periods with very little rain. They must also be able to grow in our sandy island soil.

We use plants in different ways in our yards and gardens.

The plants below are good for making hedges. To make a hedge, you trim the plant regularly into the correct shape.

▲ Cocoplum

▲ Sea grape

▲ Hibiscus

▲ Croton

Reflection

Which of these plants look familiar to you? Which other plants do you notice in your community?

▲ Buttonwood

▲ *Ficus*

Activity 1 Identify hedge plants

Match each description to one of the hedge plants on page 104.

1 Has grey-green leaves. Can be used as a shade tree or hedge. People used to use the wood for firewood, charcoal and for smoking meat and fish.

2 Large, shiny light green leaves and large trumpet-shaped flowers that are often red or yellow. The flower can also be made into a tea or cordial.

3 A shrub with round-shaped leaves. Produces a plumlike fruit. The fruit and seed are both edible. On some islands the fruit is known as 'fat pork'. The leaves and bark are used in bush medicine.

4 A bushy plant with round-shaped leaves and fruits that grow in bunches and look like grapes. You can trim it to make a tree, hedge or screen. The fruits can be made into jams, jellies and wine, and the leaves, roots and bark have some uses in bush medicine.

5 Shrub with long leaves in a variety of red, yellow and green colours. Has many different uses in bush medicine.

6 Plant with bright, glossy green leaves used to create low hedges.

We also plant different kinds of trees and shrubs to beautify our gardens, like the examples on the right.

▲ Periwinkle

▲ Yellow elder

▲ Jasmine

Activity 2 Plants in my community

1 **a** On a piece of paper, draw a table like this:

Plants used for hedges in my community	Plants used to beautify gardens and yards	Trees used in my community

b In pairs, take a walk around your neighbourhood. If possible, take photographs. Note some examples of plants that fit into each category. If you do not know the names of the plants, draw a picture or take a sample of a leaf. Try to identify them using a reference book.

c Create a class display of plants that are used for each purpose in your community. You can stick actual examples of leaves onto your display, or draw the plants. If you use digital photographs, you can make a slide show.

2 Listen to the Bahamian song 'Stay in the bush' by the Mustangs, or any other song about the flora of The Bahamas. Make up your own song about some of your local plants.

Theme 3 What have you learnt?

Unit 13 Family names

1 Write something you learnt about one of the surnames in your family or one of your friends' families in this unit.

Unit 14 Nation builders

2 Choose one nation builder you learnt about in this unit. Write a short paragraph about who they are or were, and how they contributed to our nation.

Unit 15 Junkanoo

3 What was the original name of Junkanoo?

4 Why was this festival so important during the time of slavery?

5 Look at this picture. Write a paragraph describing what it shows about the music and costumes of Junkanoo.

(Continued)

Unit 16 Holidays, festivals and regattas

6 Name each public holiday, and choose the correct date below:

(25 December)   (first Monday in August)   (the Friday before Easter Sunday)

(second Monday in October)   (first Friday in June)   (10 July)

a a day to celebrate the workers and unions

b a day when Christians celebrate the birth of Christ

c a day that commemorates the crucifixion of Christ

d a day that celebrates the freeing of enslaved people in The Bahamas

e a day that celebrates nation builders.

7 Explain in your own words what kind of event is shown in this picture, and why this event is important in The Bahamas.

Unit 17 Bahamian cuisine

8 Choose one of the traditional Bahamian dishes you learnt about. Write a riddle about it (without mentioning the name of the dish or the main ingredient). Exchange riddles with a partner and guess each other's dishes.

Unit 18 Plants of The Bahamas

9 Which of the following does a plant need to grow well in The Bahamas? Write yes or no for each item.

a round-shaped leaves

b able to grow well in sandy soil

c bright flowers

d can be trimmed into a hedge

e can survive hot summers and periods without rain.

10 Name and describe a plant that is commonly used for hedges in The Bahamas.

Glossary

A

accused: someone believed to have committed a crime

aerial view: view of an area from the air (or from directly above)

ambassador: someone who performs as a representative for their country

archaeologist: someone who studies ancient remains to put together historical records

archipelago: a collection of small islands

architecture: designed and constructed buildings

artefact: an object, usually something human-made, that tells us about a historical society or culture

atmospheric pressure: the weight with which the layer of air around the Earth pushes down on the surface

auction: a kind of sale where buyers try to outbid each other

B

bank: (of the ocean) built-up areas of carbonate deposits that cause a much shallower ocean floor

barrier reef: a coral reef that runs parallel to a coastline, so it forms a barrier between the sea that is closer to the coast and the deeper ocean

border: edge of a country or region

bottling: a process of preserving food by storing it in sealed bottles

C

cacique: chief of a Lucayan community

canning: a process of preserving food by sealing it into metal canisters

carbonate deposits: organic material formed by broken-down shells of sea animals, or mineral deposits that have precipitated from seawater

cardinal point: north, south, east and west

cargo: goods on board; a type of transportation involving goods

cartographer: someone who draws maps

citizen: a member of a specific country or nationality

climate: weather patterns of a particular place over a long period of time

coastline: the edge of a piece of land where it meets the sea

Coat of Arms: a special type of shield-shaped symbol usually for a country or family

communication: sending and receiving information

compass rose: a circular sign that shows the main directions (north, west, south and east)

conflict: a disagreement or a clash of views between people or groups

consequence: an event that happens as the result of an action or choice

Constitution: a document setting out the basic rights and principles for a country

continent: one of the large seven landmasses that makes up most of the land on Earth

country: a nation that has its own territory and government

crop farming: growing plants for food and other products

cuisine: a style of cooking, especially that of a country

D

diversity: variety or range

doctrine: a belief or set of beliefs held by a church or other institution

dugout canoe: a long, narrow sea vessel, propelled using handheld oars, typical of the Lucayans

duho: ceremonial seat used by Lucayans, usually a carved man on all fours

E

economically viable: when the economic benefits are more than the costs, for society in general

export crop: a crop grown to be sold to other countries

F

fetish: an object that people worship for its supernatural or spiritual power

field crop: a crop that grows in fields, such as cotton and sugar

field slave: an enslaved person who worked in the fields (rather than in the home)

finite: available in limited amounts that can run out

first-hand account: directly from a source

First Passage: an enslaved person's journey from their home village to the slave ships waiting at the coast

G

global event: an event that is happening in another country and making international news, or affecting the rest of the world

globe: a map presented on a 3D sphere showing the continents and countries on Earth

graphic organiser: diagram that arranges text and shapes to make information clearer

grid: a regular system of horizontal and vertical lines

guilty: responsible for a crime or a wrongful action

H

hemisphere: one half of the Earth; The Bahamas is in the northern hemisphere

harvesting: collecting a resource in order to use it

house slave

house slave: an enslaved person who worked as a servant, cook or domestic worker

human rights: a right that is believed to belong to every person

humidity: level of water vapour in the air

I

idol: an image or statue of a god

infrastructure: transport and communication networks and other structures and facilities that allow an institution or country to carry out economic activities

L

labour force: all the people who are able and willing to work in a country (including those who are unemployed)

land grant: a transfer of land ownership to a person or group

law: a set of rules decided on by parliament, to keep society functioning well

line of latitude: horizontal lines on a map (also called parallels)

line of longitude: vertical lines on a map (also called meridians)

livestock: animals that we farm for meat and other products (such as eggs and milk)

local consumption: to be sold and used in the country where they are grown

M

migrant worker: someone who travels to different places for seasonal work such as picking fruit or working on construction sites

Middle Passage: the stage in an enslaved person's journey when they would be transported from the coast of Africa to the West Indies or America in a slave ship

mind map: type of graphic organiser with a heading in the middle and smaller pieces of information around it

minerals: resources such as metals and fuels, which are found in the earth and mined

meteorologist: someone who studies the weather

N

national: relating to a country

national anthem: an uplifting song that is specific to and identified with a particular country, usually sung at formal occasions, major sports matches and ceremonies

national pride: the feeling of love for and sense of attachment to one's country

nation builder: someone who works hard to achieve very highly in their field, and who brings excellence and success to our country

natural resources: resources that occur or grow in the environment, such as soil, water and fossil fuels

P

passenger: a person on board a form of transport such as a bus or plane

patriotism: having national pride and supporting one's country

perishable: able to rot or spoil

physical map: a map that shows the natural features in an area, such as seas, rivers and mountains

plantation: large farming estate, usually for growing cash crops for export, such as sugar, coffee or cotton

plea: a statement of guilt or innocence in a court of law

pledge: a solemn promise

political map: a map showing borders and capital cities

precipitation: rain, snow, sleet or hail

preserve: to process food so that it can keep for a longer time, for example by canning or bottling

R

renewable: able to grow back or to be replaced

resource: a raw material or supply we use to meet our needs

responsibility: an obligation or duty; something we are expected to do or take care of

S

scale: a ratio that tells the relationship between the size of something represented in a model or map, and its size in real life

sea vessel: a form of transport that travels on water, such as boats and ships

sentence: when someone is found legally guilty of a crime or misdemeanour, they may receive a sentence such as a period of community service, or a term in a correctional centre

semi-renewable: needs to be regrown so it will not run out

shelf life: how long a food item can last

source: in history, a source is a person, object or record that provides information directly from a particular time or event

spoilage: rotting

stopover visitor: a tourist who stays over one or more nights

sustainable: able to continue without running out

T

tourist: someone who travels to another region or country to visit

transportation: ways of travelling from one place to another

transatlantic slave trade: the organised kidnapping and trafficking of people from Africa to bring them to work as enslaved people in European colonies

triangular slave trade: another term for the transatlantic slave trade, which focused on the three-way transport of goods and people between the West Indies, USA and Europe

U

unified: make or become united

uprising: an act of coordinated resistance against a government or master

V

visa: a document granting permission to enter a country

W

weather: the state of the atmosphere at a particular time: how hot, cold, cloudy, windy, wet or dry it is

workforce: the group of people currently employed within the labour force